Twayne's United States Authors Series

Sylvia E. Bowman, *Editor*

INDIANA UNIVERSITY

Thomas Nelson Page

THOMAS NELSON PAGE

by **THEODORE L. GROSS**
The City College of New York

Twayne Publishers, Inc. :: New York

To Selma

Preface

MORE THAN ANY OTHER WRITER in late nineteenth-century American literature, Thomas Nelson Page is associated with the plantation tradition, with the recrudescence of an ideal way of life that vanished with the Civil War and Reconstruction. In his finest fiction, he recalls a golden age: a time of stability when the South was agrarian and self-contained and when the ruler of the land was the great white planter. Page created a myth that embodied only those characteristics of ante-bellum life he wished to remember; but he projected that myth in forceful, compelling legends which persuaded a generation of readers of their author's accuracy and which still linger in the popular mind even though Page's fiction is rarely read today.

Page was a local-color writer with a limited though delicate and often impressive talent. His one contribution to American letters—the evocation of life in Virginia before the Civil War—still remains a standard of its kind. In its own time its influence on Southern writers was widespread and great. "It is hard to explain in simple terms," wrote Grace King in her memoirs, "what Thomas Nelson Page meant to us in the South at that time. He was the first Southern writer to appear in print as a Southerner, and his stories, short and simple, written in Negro dialect, and I may say, Southern pronunciation, showed us with ineffable grace that although we were sore bereft, politically, we had now a chance in literature at least."[1]

So typical a statement testifies to Page's historical and esthetic significance, the large and pervasive effect that he had on his contemporaries. Indeed, few critics and scholars of his time—Northern as well as Southern—questioned Page's crucial role in American literary history; he was in many ways the literary spokesman of the South during the 1880's and 1890's. The early stories of *In Ole Virginia* and the essays collected in *The Old South, The Old Dominion,* and *The Negro: the Southerner's Problem* represented for the general reader the traditional view of the conservative Southerner. As spokesman, Page attempted to reconcile the two sections in all that he wrote; he claimed in the preface to his collected works that he had "never wittingly written a line which he did not hope might tend to bring about a better understanding between the North and the South, and finally lead to a more perfect Union."[2] But, sincere as Page was, his fiction demonstrates that the absolute commitment to the myth of Southern heroism, to a certain rigid attitude toward the Negro and to all Southern problems, made political if not literary reconciliation quiet impossible.

For today's reader, Page's significance is two-fold: first, as the creator of a collection of compelling stories that evoke the old South, that re-create in idealistic and sentimental though poignant terms plantation life as it might have been before the Civil War; and, second, as the most lucid and impressive chronicler of a myth of heroism that reveals one dominant Southern attitude toward the Negro. I have concentrated on these two aspects of Page's work. The first three chapters deal with the development of Page's tragedy of the South, and I analyze and evaluate his most memorable writing: the stories of *In Ole Virginia*, the essays on race, and the novel *Red Rock*. The last three chapters trace Page's attempt to emerge from his Southern past and apply his attitudes to the contemporary problems that attended a growing industrialism.

Page could not reconcile his inherited assumptions with the changing demands of the twentieth-century world; but this ideological recalcitrance, as expressed in his small yet significant artistic achievement, illuminates an aspect of the Southern imagination rarely provided by other writers whose attitudes were more ambivalent and complex. The problems of racial tension today find their roots in the world that Thomas Nelson Page dramatizes. More representative perhaps than any postbellum Southern author of the nineteenth century, Page preserved a plantation legend that "dominated Southern fiction half a century after it took shape in the 1800's" and still "is by no means dead."[3]

This book is the first full-length study of Thomas Nelson Page that has been published. Most of the commentaries on his work have been sentimental and affectionate—his brother's biography, published in 1923, is a good example—and were written early in the century without regard for scholarly standards. Page occupies chapters in more recent, reputable literary histories like Jay B. Hubbell's *The South in American Literature* (1954) and Edmund Wilson's *Patriotic Gore* (1962), where he is given judicious treatment. But the only complete account of his life and work is an unpublished dissertation by Harriet Holman, written for Duke University in 1947. I am deeply indebted to Miss Holman for the abundant and accurate information she has furnished; without her help, this pleasant task would have been far more onerous.

I would like to thank the editors of *The Georgia Review* for permitting me to reprint parts of my essay, "Thomas Nelson Page: Creator of a Virginia Classic," which appeared in the Fall, 1966 issue of that journal.

THEODORE L. GROSS

The City College of New York
New York City
November, 1965

Contents

Chronology

1853   Thomas Nelson Page was born on April 23, in Oakland, Hanover County, Virginia, the son of John Page and Elizabeth Burwell Nelson Page.

1869   In September, Page entered Washington and Lee College, Lexington, Virginia, where Robert E. Lee was president. He never graduated, leaving in June, 1872.

1872   Because he lacked the funds for law school, Page tutored the children of Theodore Brown in Louisville, Kentucky.

1873   He studied law at the University of Virginia, living economically with his aunt. He joined the Jefferson Literary Society and wrote for *The Virginia University Magazine*.

1874   In November Page passed his bar and practiced law in the Hanover circuit until 1876.

1876   He moved to Richmond and practiced law with his cousin. "Uncle Gabe's White Folks," a dialect poem sold to *Scribner's Monthly*; appeared in April, 1877. In June he was given a commission to report Ralph Waldo Emerson's Charlottesville address for the *Richmond Enquirer*.

1881   Page sold "Marse Chan" to the *Century* magazine. It was published in March, 1884, and was followed in 1886 by "Unc' Edinburg's Drowndin'," "Meh Lady," and "Ole 'Stracted."

1885   He went into a law partnership with his kinsman, Thomas Nelson Carter, with whom he practiced until 1893.

1886   On July 28, Page married Anne Seddon Bruce, and they took a wedding trip to England and the Continent. She died of a throat hemorrhage four days before Christmas, 1888.

1887   *In Ole Virginia, or Marse Chan and Other Stories.*

1888 *Befo' de War* and *Two Little Confederates.*

1890 Page traveled to England to sell the Duluth land in which he had invested, but was not successful. Began a series of lecture tours, reading from *In Ole Virginia* and delivering essays such as "The Old South" and "Literature in the South Before the War."

1891 *Among the Camps; Elsket and Other Stories; On New-found River.*

1892 *The Old South.* In Chicago, Page met Mrs. Florence Lathrop Field, widowed sister-in-law of Marshall Field.

1893 Page married Mrs. Field. He gave up his law practice and moved from Richmond to Washington, becoming a fashionable man of the city.

1894 *The Burial of the Guns* and *Pastime Stories.*

1897 *The Old Gentleman of the Black Stock.*

1898 *Red Rock; Two Prisoners.*

1899 *Santa Claus's Partner.*

1902 *A Captured Santa Claus.*

1903 *Gordon Keith.*

1904 *Bred in the Bone.*

1906 *A Coast of Bohemia.*

1907 *Under the Crust.*

1908 *The Old Dominion; Tommy Trot's Visit to Santa Claus; Robert E. Lee, Southerner;* revised and published as *Robert E. Lee, Man and Soldier,* in 1911.

1908- *The Novels, Stories, Sketches, and Poems of Thomas*
1912 *Nelson Page.* The Plantation Edition, eighteen volumes.

1912 The Plantation Edition, eighteen volumes.

1909 *John Marvel, Assistant.*

1910 Because of ill health, Page spent the winter in Cuba.

1912 Page was active in the presidential campaign, first working against Wilson's nomination and then supporting him as a candidate.

1913 He was appointed ambassador to Italy by Woodrow

Wilson and served for six years. On August 13, he sailed
for Rome. *The Land of the Spirit.*

1920 *Italy and the World War.* He traveled to England to be
with his sick daughter, Minna.

1921 Mrs. Page died in Southboro, Massachusetts, at the house
of her daughter, Florence. Page traveled to the Midwest
and delivered various lectures, most of which concerned
Dante. These essays later appeared as *Dante and His
Influence.* Page made a trip with his brother Rosewell to
"refresh his memory as to the scenes and incidents of the
Hampton 'Red Shirt Campaign' for his novel, *The Red
Riders.*"

1922 *Dante and His Influence.* Page died on November 1, at
Oakland.

1923 *Washington and Its Romance.*

1924 *The Red Riders;* the last sections of this novel were
written by Page's brother, Rosewell.

CHAPTER 1

The Myth of Southern Heroism

THE GENERATIONS of Pages and Nelsons that settled in
Virginia in the early eighteenth century are of special
significance in any study of Thomas Nelson Page, for they form
the background to his fiction—the historical legacy he dramatically champions and defends. From Page's point of view these
generations of heroic figures lived through a golden age, and
their way of life is the moral criterion against which he contrasts the decline and fall of social stability in the Reconstruction era.

In 1730 Page's ancestor, after having graduated from Eton,
came to America and established himself in Gloucester County,
Virginia. He built Rosewell, a plantation home which was the
largest in the state. As Page recalls the mansion in his various
essays on colonial Virginia, he invests it with historical grandeur: Rosewell was the site where Pocahontas intervened for
John Smith, and the house where Thomas Jefferson wrote and
showed the Declaration of Independence to his friend John
Page, grandson of the original settler. John Page of Rosewell,
as the Revolutionary leader was known, had inherited a fortune
and was famous throughout the state as a "member of Congress,
and governor of Virginia."[1] But he "was financially so involved
at his death in 1808" that the mansion had to be sold.

"The Nelson family had been importers and shipowners since
'Scotch Tom' Nelson settled at Yorktown about 1705; the war of
1812 ruined family business and consumed most of its wealth
when the Nelson warehouses were burned at Yorktown."[2] Both
families were "Virginia cavaliers," but they had had little money
since the beginning of the nineteenth century; their later
historian, Thomas Nelson Page, was deeply sensitive about this
fact.

Page's father, John Page, was the sixth of seven children. The family could not afford to send him to the University of Virginia or to William and Mary, and he stayed with his brother-in-law in Pennsylvania while attending an Episcopal school; later he taught for a year in a high school and earned enough money to enter the University of Virginia in 1843. After graduating, he became a well-respected lawyer in Hanover County; but he never prospered, and his son grew up amidst very modest circumstances.

Born on April 23, 1853, Page experienced a quiet, rural boyhood in Hanover County until the Civil War. His father owned land and some sixty slaves, but his Oakland plantation was very small—a good description of it, and of Page's youthful excursions in the war, appears in *Two Little Confederates* (1888). Although no battle was "fought in the immediate vicinity of Oakland," Hanover County was the site of "McClellan's campaign of 1862 and Grant's campaign of 1864"; the "whole area was in effect a battlefield."[3]

With the war as a background to his boyhood adventures, he grew up in a large and intimate family. His conservative parents implanted in the young boy not only a strict religious faith— Page's mother insisted on prayer three times a day—but also a deep suspicion that political or social change meant an inevitable decline in moral values. This latter attitude becomes particularly significant in his work, as the titles of his various books suggest: *In Ole Virginia, Social Life in Old Virginia, The Old Dominion;* and it caused him to glorify the past to so great a degree that any present world—and especially the world of Reconstruction—was a decline from that peaceful time before the war.

Page's education was desultory. The greatest personal influence on him was that of his father, who "among all the men the writer knew in his youth was the most familiar with books; and who of all the men the writer has ever known has exemplified best the virtue of open-handedness."[4] He first attended his aunt's day school at Oakland, where he learned enough Latin to read Virgil; but his education there was interrupted at various times and not seriously continued until he studied with a relative whose sister, affectionately called Cousin Fanny, introduced him to the poetry of Tennyson and the fiction of Scott. Scott was of great importance to Page, and at this time he read the Waverley novels. Never strongly motivated in terms of a formal education, he left Washington College, which he had entered in 1869, without graduating. "I neglected my studies shamefully," he recollected in later life, "and got through [each semester] in the class of damnable mediocrity."⁵

Page was poor and hated his poverty. He had no money for the law degree he wanted and was compelled, therefore, to tutor the children of his cousins, a Brown family that lived outside of Louisville, Kentucky. After having earned enough money, he returned to Virginia to study law at the University of Virginia. He took an "active part in debates of the Jefferson Literary Society" and wrote for *The Virginia University Magazine;*⁶ as a student, he was never very effective. In the strain of studying for his oral examinations, he suffered a breakdown the day before he was to be tested. In November, 1874, however, he successfully passed the examinations and practiced law during the next two years in the Hanover circuit. Soon he joined the Richmond Club and became a well-known, reliable young lawyer in Richmond society. He also did some incidental writing for newspapers and once elicited the rancor of Ralph Waldo Emerson, whose Charlottesville address Page reported for the *Richmond Enquirer.*⁷

Law was the profession most Southern authors first pursued, and Page's attitude toward the profession and toward literature was typical. At the outset and until 1893, when he gave up his law practice entirely, he treated writing as though it were avocational. "I have often been asked how I came to be a writer," he remarks in *Recollections and Reflections,* "and I wonder myself, especially when I see instances of men who have set themselves to become writers just as I set out to be a lawyer. I think the principal thing after my liking for books, was my desire to see myself in print. Emulation of others, the desire to add to my poor income, and ambition all afterwards played their part; but I think . . . the first motive was, to use a term for want of a better—vanity."⁸

This reason is casual and common enough; but, whatever the initial impetus, in a short time he found himself seriously engaged as an author, and for many reasons other than vanity. He discovered, for one thing, that he was expressing the sentiments of many writers, that he was in effect a leader of the whole Southern school of local-color fiction. As such, he assumed the burden of defending the South against its critics and, at the same time, of reconciling the differences between North and South. He fixed in the imagination of Northerners, as well as of Southerners, the plantation tradition; and he dedicated himself creatively to representing the South to the nation in the most idealistic manner.

His first published work was a dialect poem, "Uncle Gabe's White Folks," written in 1876 and published in *Scribner's Monthly* in April, 1877. As Page confessed, the poem was strongly influenced by Irwin Russell's early dialect verse, especially "Christmas Night in the Quarters" (1876): "It was the light of Russell's genius shining through his dialect poems—first of dialect poems and still first—that led my feet in the direction I have since tried to follow."[9] "Uncle Gabe's White Folks" established the Negro point of view and dialect that were to prove so effective in the fine stories that soon followed.

> "Sarvent, Marster! Yes, suh, dat's me
> Ole Unc' Gabe's my name."

As in "Marse Chan" and "Unc' Edinburg's Drowndin'," this faithful Negro recalls for his white listener the glories of plantation life, the myth of the Great House where the white lady's silk dress seemed to "talk" and where the Master's smile was all the Negro needed to be happy:

> "Live mons'ous high?" Yes, Marster, yes;
> D' cut 'n' onroyal 'n' gordly dash;
> Eat and drink till you could n' res',
> My folks war n' none o' yo po'-white-trash;
> Nor, suh, dey was of high degree—
> Dis heah nigger am quality! (X, 293)

After recounting the various characteristics of the plantation, Uncle Gabe discovers that his listener is actually his master, who has returned to purchase the land and the house; thus, in an extravagant flourish, the slave's wish is realized. Page avoids this sentimental excess in his stories, which usually conclude with the unfulfilled longing of the Negro (as in "Ole 'Stracted") or with the romantic death of the Southern hero (as in "Marse Chan," "Unc' Edinburg's Drowndin'," and "Meh Lady"). Death, the dominant note struck in the stories of *In Ole Virginia*, comes to symbolize the historical passing of the old order and takes on a poignance that is suited to the decline of a civilization.

Page tries to evoke in his early stories the sense of an oral tradition which suggests that the speaker is the last survivor of the romantic plantation, one who is fixing for all time the way life was in the South before the Civil War. His method of composition mirrored the tonal effects he searched for: "first, he told the story over and over to one friend after another until the reaction of his listeners showed him that it was effective; then he wrote it; and finally, he read the story to neighbors, his Sunday school class, or a lecture audience, skipping over passages which caused his listener's interest to lag."[10]

The method is almost entirely successful in those stories he included in *In Ole Virginia* (1887): in them one sees the code of Southern heroism function in a ritualistic form that is perfectly suited to Page's evocation of the past; and one witnesses too the culmination of a sentimental tradition that dominates nineteenth-century Southern literature. The code of Southern heroism had long been central to ante-bellum Southern writing, and one finds aspects of it in the fiction of John P. Kennedy (in *Swallow Barn*), William A. Caruthers (in *The Cavaliers of Virginia*), John Esten Cooke, William Gilmore Simms, and many others. Page sees the code in retrospect as the armature of a great and fallen civilization: more than any of these authors, he raises the code to mythical proportions. His heroes must learn to live by the code—most of the stories that will now be considered are basically concerned with that process of learning; his Negroes admire only those whites who enforce the code; and his ladies insist upon the hero's demonstration of it before they submit themselves in marriage.

The code of Southern heroism involves a moral attitude in which truth and honor and loyalty are constant; a military discipline in which fencing and riding and hunting are necessary accomplishments; and an inflexible social posture that represents the quintessence of manners, courtesy, and hospitality. Other characteristics of the code that inevitably develop as the hero matures are the idealization of woman, which, as W. J. Cash has suggested, amounts to "gyneolatry"; extravagant oratory; a sectional chauvinism, which flowers into Southern nationalism; a great emphasis on heraldry and ancestry, and the consequent glorification of the past; and, finally, a desire to establish a political state like that of Pericles' Athens, a "free state based on a slave proletariat."[11]

Page adheres to this code so rigidly that his best fiction—the stories of *In Ole Virginia* (1887)—takes on the qualities of epic; the reader feels that his heroes and heroines, who are given ideal dimensions, are perpetuating the noble qualities of a great race.

I *"Marse Chan": The Southern Gentleman*

The origins of "Marse Chan" are significant, for as Page remembers them in the Preface to his Collected Works, they prepare the reader for the mythical and sentimental world that he is entering; they condition the mind of the reader to a certain way of thinking:

> In the autumn of 1880 a letter was shown [to Page] which had been taken from the pocket of a dead private in a Georgia regiment on one of the battle-fields around Richmond. It was written in an illiterate hand on coarse blue Confederate paper, and was from a young girl in Georgia to her sweetheart. In it she told him that she had discovered since he left that she loved him, and that she did not know why she had been so cruel to him before he went away; that, in fact, she had loved him ever since they had gone to school together in the little school-house in the woods, when he had been so good to her and that now if he would get a furlough and come home she would marry him. This was all, except, of course, a postscript. As if fearful that such a temptation might prove too much even for the man she loved, across the blue Confederate paper were scrawled these words: "Don't come without a furlough; for if you don't come honorable, I won't marry you."[12]

The soldier dies in battle—"he got his furlough through a bullet"—and Page remarks that the "idea took possession of me, and in about ten days I had written 'Marse Chan.' This story was promptly accepted, but was not published until something over three years afterwards. It was then followed by the other stories in 'In Ole Virginia,' and later by the remaining tales in this edition."[13]

The ingredients of the Southern local-color story—honor, loyalty, love, the dangers of battle, death, the evocative past that the hero and the heroine have shared—are all present in this incident upon which "Marse Chan" is based; and they

are completely compatible with Page's own interest in Southern literature and life. All that the author needs to convert life
into literature is the proper and authentic point of view. In
choosing the slave as narrator, he gives his story its most
memorable quality, a voice that is a haunting and convincing
echo, which, like the chorus of Greek tragedy, judges and
interprets as well as reports the tragedy. Furthermore, the
Negro narrator frees Page from "the necessity of being specific";
he is a "spectator rather than a participant in the action" and
can "therefore relate the whole story without either obvious
self-glorification or undue reticence."[14] By using a Negro narrator, the author successfully creates his idyll, a sentimentalized
past which no one can refute; for the Negro—romantic, superstitious, and nostalgic—summons up that past with complete
recall: he was there; and if at times he seems a bit of a *voyeur*
with a phenomenal memory, he is credible as the witness of
that vanished era of glory.[15]

Sam, the Negro, tells his story to a white man who may be
Southern or Northern—the reader is never certain—who may be
Page himself or the reader. This man meets the isolated Negro
in the post-bellum South—the time is the autumn of 1872—and
sees a shattered, disoriented ex-slave suffering the horrors of
Reconstruction. Cleverly, Page puts the reader in the position of
the author as someone listening objectively to recorded history,
a history that takes on special significance since Sam is the
only survivor of the wasted plantation and now bears the
burden of accuracy.

Although the general outline of the story has been given to
him, Page wants the reader to feel the full pathos of his hero's
death, and he provides a background—what is to be the archetypical background for all his Southern fiction—to Marse Chan's
life. Seen from the point of view of the Negro Sam, this life is
highly ritualistic. It is even mythical; for in Page's eyes the
development of the Southern hero, the boy who will later
defend a civilization, the innocent youth who must learn and
adhere to the code of Southern heroism, is as impressive as that
of any knight in King Arthur's court.

Chan's birth is a time of great festivity—"jes' like in de
Chris'mas," the narrator remembers—and the author makes it
clear that this birth, like that of Christ, is holy and significant.
Eventually the reader discovers that the boy is a martyr to the

Southern cause, someone crucified in a war that for Page was as religious and moral as it was civil. The father, when he gives his infant son a body servant, elects the Negro boy Sam for that sacred role, thus promoting a love relationship between the two that stems from birth. Throughout childhood the white and Negro boys attend school together, although, as Sam quickly assures his listener, only Marse Chan studies. Sam assumes his servile condition; indeed, he is proud of it and wears his slavery like a badge of honor and distinction. He is no rebellious, discontent slave but a servant who is happy to share his master's life and who feels that his own status is enhanced by his close relationship to Marse Chan. As Sam remembers the ante-bellum period, he pictures it in glowing terms: "Dem wuz good ole times, marster—de bes' Sam ever see. Dey wuz, in fac'! Niggers didn' hed nothin' 't all to do—jes' hed to 'ten' to de feedin' an' cleanin' de hosses, an' doin' what de marster tell 'em to do; an' when dey wuz sick, dey had things sont 'em out de house, an' de same doctor come to see 'em whar 'ten' to de white folks when dey wez po'ly. Dyar warn' no trouble nor nothin'" (I, 13).

Plantation life, described in its rural splendor, is a fit setting for the development of the Southern hero. What the reader witnesses in this early part of the story is the moral education of a young boy, the tender details of a *bildungsroman*. Marse Chan not only learns formally in the school but also discovers how a Southerner must act in society. His early romance with Anne Chamberlain, the daughter of his father's political rival, is marked by a chivalric, deferential attitude; his loyalty to his body servant is unwavering; his defense of his father's honor remains constant. Chivalry, loyalty, honor, heroism: these traits equip Chan for the duel which forms the central conflict of the story.

Chan's father is a democrat and Anne Chamberlain's a Whig; though both are loyal Southerners and eventually join forces against the North, Chan's father—like all Page's sympathetic characters—is opposed to secession and the extreme political measures of the Whigs. He buys slaves that Chamberlain sells, thus embittering the conservative. When a barn burns and a Negro, in trying to save the horses, is trapped in the flames, old Marse Chan rescues the Negro; but in demonstrating his instinctive loyalty and love for one who has served him, he blinds himself. This episode is made more dramatic "because of the narrator's complete absence of comment." To the slave, "the 'marster' had a right to send his slave into danger, but that implied a duty to save him in turn, even if it cost his owner his eyesight."[16] His son, who has now learned the code of Southern heroism and who has adopted his father's political and social beliefs, carries on the family traditions; he challenges Chamberlain's political ideas and, consequently, the man. Insults inevitably occur, for these men are Southern firebrands, and they meet in that ancient chivalric contest—the duel.

For Chan the duel takes on religious connotations. As the Negro narrator remarks, Chan "look like he did sometimes when he come out of church." He is fighting for honor, and honor for Page always has a religious dimension. Furthermore, the duel is not so frivolous as a modern reader might believe, for it grows out of the central political conflict between Southerners in ante-bellum times; it reflects the tensions that will inevitably lead to the Civil War and reminds one of the divergent political views of many Southerners. Esthetically, Page is imitating Scott's *Ivanhoe*, but he is grafting onto the duel a political and historical meaning of particular significance. Chamberlain misses his opponent, and Chan generously fires in the air. But there is no resolution to the conflict between these feuding families; and, as in the story of Romeo and Juliet, the victims are the lovers who must remain apart.

Page attempts to weld realistic and romantic elements in his legend. The war would ordinarily give a historical validity to otherwise trivial, sentimental situations; but the Civil War that Page describes seems enjoyable, or at least romantic, rather than onerous—it is an adventure, almost a *jeu d'esprit*. Page's Civil War is not that described by De Forest in *Miss Ravenel's Conversion from Secession to Loyalty*. The comparison is apt: De Forest experienced the war, Page writes at second hand; he writes after having experienced the humiliation of Reconstruction, and he imagines experiences that took place when he was a boy of eight. Marse Chan as a Southern hero is a boyhood projection, a fanciful surrogate that Page imagines for himself. "*He* 'peared to like to go prowlin' aroun' 'mong dem Yankees," the narrator says, "an' he use' to tek me wid 'im whenever he could. Yes, seh, he sut'n'y wuz a good sodger! He didn' mine bullets no more 'n he did so many drops o' rain. But I use' to be pow'ful skeered sometimes. It jes use' to 'pear like fun to 'im" (I, 35).

Privately, Chan grieves the loss of Anne Chamberlain in good chivalric fashion. His lady, like the lady of medieval legend— or of Scott's version of it—rebuffs him; the lover, though morbidly melancholy, does not question her judgment—she is, after all, a moral arbiter, an absolute spiritual criterion against which he measures his own inadequate self. Anne Chamberlain symbolizes Southern purity and innocence, qualities that are almost mystical and certainly beyond definition in Page's moral universe.

The conclusion of the story is sentimentally contrived but nevertheless poignant. Anne Chamberlain sends Chan a letter in which she confesses her love: immediately after he has read the letter, Chan dies on the battlefield—heroically, of course— and his Negro body servant, loving him in death as well as in life, makes his coffin, places him in it, and takes him home. The Negro's love for his white master is the most moving aspect of "Marse Chan," the characteristic that gives the story its verisimilitude and uniqueness.

The relationship between Anne Chamberlain and Marse Chan is more artificial because Page must keep his heroine so incredibly idealistic that she is not human. She loves Chan in death; in death, she can even dare to be erotic: "Miss Anne she tuk de coffin in her arms an' kissed it, an' kissed Marse Chan, an' call 'im by his name, an' her darlin', an' ole missis lef' her cryin' in dyar tell some on 'em went in, an' found her done faint on de flo'" (I, 44). She dies and thus remains pristine and innocent, her abstract attributes never threatened by the practicalities of the post-Civil War South. She and her lover are buried together—"dey's bofe in en sleep side over de ole grabeyard at home."

The only credible person in this story—and in those that follow—is the Negro. The other characters belong to a mythical past that cannot be realistically created because it is not real; it is the author's evocation, his "picture of a civilization which, once having sweetened the life of the South, has since then well-nigh perished from the earth." (I, vii). Page, as Jay B. Hubbell points out, was among the first to see that "the old life was passing away"; he is clearly responding to a deep need that he shared with other Southerners: "The later South wanted its heroes painted, not as provincial tobacco farmers but as heroes and Cavaliers. . . . There is just the difference between [Page's] Virginia and the real Virginia that one expects to find between a painting and a photograph. Certain details of the old life are dropped or barely mentioned; while others are emphasized in every possible manner."[17]

Still, as idealistic as one may feel the author's fictional past to be—and even Southern writers like Mary Johnston and J. B. Cabell refuted his version—there is little doubt that of all those Southern authors who depicted plantation life, Page is most effective: "*In Ole Virginia* is preeminently the Virginia classic."[18] John P. Kennedy, William A. Caruthers, Beverly Tucker, and John Esten Cooke had all portrayed plantation life, but Page re-creates the period as though he is recording history. He gives this pre-war world majesty and dignity, and he persuades the reader to his belief: in the death of his Southern hero is implied the death of a civilization—a heroic period, a Golden Age "when men treated women chivalrously and women relied on men implicitly, when success bore no relation to wealth, and when the seventh commandment was not deemed a proper subject for conversation in mixed company" (I, viii).

II   *"Unc' Edinburg's Drowndin': A Plantation Echo"*

Nostalgia for this heroic time, when the moral order of the South was stable, is the real subject of "Unc' Edinburg's Drowndin'." The subtitle, A "Plantation Echo," accurately describes this evocation of the past. Page attaches a story to his memory of ante-bellum life, but it is largely contrived and insignificant. What emerges as memorable is "the social life of the South when it was somewhat distinctive"; he records, again through the eyes of the slave, a moment of history, a time of stability and moral health, that is implicitly contrasted with the present degradation of the South during Reconstruction.

The action centers on an unconsummated love affair. The lovers, Charlotte and George, are separated as in "Marse Chan" by the divergent political views of their families. The heroine's stepbrother is George's political opponent, and the two men debate publicly. Much of the story is concerned with the rhetorical performances of the two men, and Page, through his Negro narrator, dramatizes the condition of politics in pre-war Virginia: " 'lections wuz 'lections dem days; dee warn' no bait-gode 'lections, wid ev'y sort o 'worms squirmin' up 'ginst one nurr, wid piece o' paper d'ain' know what on, drappin' in a chink; didn' nuttin' but gent'mens vote den, an' dee took dee dram, an' vote out loud, like gent'mens" (I, 71). Page, in *Red Rock* and *The Red Riders,* describes in detail "the changes which war and war's bastard offspring, Reconstruction, have brought about" (I, xi); but in these early stories he concentrates on ante-bellum times when only gentlemen voted. He is content to imply the later world of politics made corrupt by venal carpetbaggers.

The lovers of the story are never united in life because the hero contracts a fatal illness when he saves the narrator, Uncle Edinburg, from drowning. But in death the lovers are spiritually joined: the heroine, Charlotte, is told that

> "she got to come, ef she don't, he'll die dat night; an' fust thing I know, Miss Lucy bring Miss Charlotte in, wid her face right white, but jes as tender as a angel's, an' she come an' stan' by de side de bed, an' lean down over him, an' call he name, 'George!' —jes so.
> "An Marse George he ain' answer: he jes look at her study for a minute, an' den he forehead get 'smooth, an' he tun he eyes to me, an' say, 'Edinburg, I'm 'cross." (I, 93-94)

The hero dies, his love spiritually if not physically consummated. Once again the two main characters are types: the Southern hero and his lady; once again the Negro slave, with his humor and deviltry and human foibles, is more credible than his master. The merits of the story lie in Page's re-creation of plantation life—as he thought it had existed. The depiction of the rural landscape, the celebration of Christmas, the loyalty and closeness of Negro and white ("my mammy," Uncle Edinburg reports, " 'nussed us bofe at one breast"), the social and political attitudes before the Civil War—these characteristics make "Unc' Edinburg's Drowndin'" one of those many local-color stories that freeze a moment of history, that animate in a unique way one special area of the country. "The portrayal here," Arlin Turner suggests, "employs double reflecting sur-faces: the Negroes as the whites imagine them look at the whites as the whites want to appear and as they appear to the Negroes. The result in Page is a fascinating portrayal of both whites and blacks of the plantation era, however unreal they may be."[19]

"Unc' Edinburg's Drowndin'" is perhaps the most typical story that Page wrote, the one that best represents his distinctive qualities. This story alone "crowds into its few pages virtually all the significant elements of the social rapture which marked the old epoch; all of life's splendors, its joys, and, at the same time, the unique cordiality that marked race relations. Page's portrayals remain the standard of plantation literature."[20] He himself recognized the uniqueness of the tale in a letter that he wrote to Arthur Hobson Quinn: "Personally I have always estimated 'Edinburg's Drowndin' as possibly the broadest of my stories, at least as the one giving a reflection of the broadest current of the old Southern life, and so far as literary art is concerned, it seems to me at least on a par with the others."[21]

III *"Meh Lady": Sectional Reconciliation*

"Meh Lady" (1886) does not depend so exclusively on local color as "Unc' Edinburg's Drowndin'." Page tells a story of reconciliation—so common in the popular literature of post-bellum times—and through the ceremonial death of his hero and the desperate dignity of his heroic sister, he implies the tragedy of the South: the fall of a higher civilization. The story is impressive in its legendary, mythical overtones: more is suggested than is realistically stated, and the reader feels that he is witnessing an enormous drama being played for the last time. The Negro narrator, Billy, watches the South before, during, and after the war and reports his tragedy with what impresses the reader as faithful accuracy.

This tale—more than any other in *In Ole Virginia*— is written with Page's audience in mind: it is an archetypical story of reconciliation, a conscious model for later local-color writers. The idea of the story was suggested by Robert Underwood Johnson, the editor of the *Century*, who had been "reading Lessing's 'Minna von Barnhelm,' in which a Prussian hero wooed a Saxon heroine in the interest of a united Germany." As Paul H. Buck notes, "It matters little. The alchemy was Page. 'Meh Lady' was a fresh creation in which the baser metals of sectional strife were transmuted into pure gold. A later generation may deem it insignificant but in the eighties it was one of the brightest ornaments of reconciliation."[22] And reconciliation was one of the author's chief aims, not only in this story but in all his fiction. As he states in the Introduction to the Plantation Edition, he "feels that he may without impropriety claim that with his devotion for the South, whose life he has tried faithfully to portray, and his pride in the Union, which he has rejoiced to see fully restored in his time, he has never wittingly written a line which he did not hope might tend to bring about a better understanding between the North and the South, and finally lead to a more perfect Union" (I, xi).

"Meh Lady" is full of the pathos so necessary to the tale of sectional reconciliation. The Southern hero grows up with his sister on a plantation that has been affluent. After college, the boy prepares for war and rides off to defend his homeland: "when Marse Phil fetch he s'o'de home an' put on he boots an' spurs whar I done black, an' git he seat on Palandin' twarn' nay han' on de place but what say Marse Phil 'bleeged to whup 'em ef dee come close enough. Well, so he went off to de war . . ." (I, 101-2). Marse Phil is killed in the war and his sister, now Meh Lady, goes to claim his body: "Dee [the Army officials] sort o' reason wid her, but she jes' walk on by wid her head up, an' tell me to foller her, an' dat I did, mon! an' lef' 'en dyah in de road holdin' dee gun. De whole army couldn' 'a 'keep her fum Marse Phil den" (I, 107). Page gives Meh Lady an indomitable will, and she, virginal yet tenacious, takes on the purity, nobility, and strength of Southern womanhood. She has no name throughout the story, for she is larger and more significant than any single human being; her traits of courage and stoicism, dignity and loyalty, are identified with all Southern women.[23] Her brother Phil symbolizes the old South itself, and his death is that of a romantic civilization: "An' when we got home Mistis [the hero's mother] she had de coffin brought in, and cyared him in he own room while we waitin', and she set in dyah all day long wid him, and he look like a boy sleepin' dyah so young, in little gray jacket wid he s'o'de 'cross he breas'" (I, 108-9).

With the death of the Southern master, the plantation falls into decline, although mother and daughter make an attempt to maintain it. Northerners, who occupy the home, ravage it, and the women are left defenseless—until the gentle and heroic Northern captain reprimands the men and then assumes personal responsibility for protection of the house. It is important to note that the new hero, whose name Wilton suggests the acquiescence that a reasonable Northern man is required to make in a tale of reconciliation, is half-Virginian; his Southern background is at least partially responsible for his instinctive knowledge of the code of behavior, the code of Southern heroism. In other stories and novels—most notably in *Red Rock*—Northerners who travel South become either rapacious villains or converted Southerners; there is no intermediary position for a character in Page's fiction.

Wilton is wounded in his defense of the house, and Meh Lady nurses him in her brother's room, on her brother's bed—the obviousness of his conversion need not be demonstrated. This incident seems a natural enough scene with which to conclude the story, for reconciliation has been completely effected; but Meh Lady finds that she cannot marry a Union soldier, and he leaves. These last pages of the story—filled with the stark poverty and simple dignity of Southerners—are among the most effective in Page's fiction because they are the least pretentious. He has a natural tendency to sentimentalize all his material, and the saccharine approach often disqualifies whatever idea he is presenting. But in "Meh Lady" the feeling is genuine, rooted as it is in historical truth. Page does not have to elaborate on conditions that actually existed in his own boyhood.

In the midst of the post-war desolation, Meh Lady teaches Negroes—although the Negroes themselves protest—and sacrifices herself to all those on her ruined plantation. Sternly she refuses the hand of her Northern lover, but in the end she capitulates to his kindness and to the imprecations of the Negroes who serve her. North and South are reconciled in a marriage that everybody celebrates. The powerful sections of the story—in which the Southern lady suffers the degradation of defeat and in which she sees personal possessions traded for the money they will command and the plantation itself sold—are marred by Page's sentimental ending. In it he is obviously pandering to Northern and Southern audiences alike, trying faithfully "to bring about a better understanding between the North and South." The last page of this story is worth quoting in full, for it suggests the best and the worst in Page's writing;

it captures all those characteristics—pathos, sentimentality, the idealization of an imagined way of life—for which Page is remembered:

> An' when de preacher git to dat part whar ax who give dis woman to de man, he sort o' wait an' he eye sort o' rove to me disconfused like he ax me ef I know; an' I don' know huccome 'twuz, but I think 'bout Marse Jeems an' Mistis when he ax me dat, an' Marse Phil, whar all dead, an' all de scufflin' we done been th'oo, an' how de chile ain' got nobody to teck her part now 'cept jes' me; and now, when he wait an' look at me dat way, an' ax me dat, I 'bleeged to speak up, I jes' step for'ard an' say: "Gord."
>
> An' jes' den de sun crawl roun' de winder shetter an' res' on her like it pourin' light all over her.
>
> An' dat night when de preacher was gone wid he wife, an' Hannah done drapt off to sleep, I wuz settin' in de do' wid meh pipe, an' I heah 'em settin' dyah on de front steps, dee voices soun'in low like bees, an' de moon sort o' meltin' over de yard, an' I sort o' got to studyin', an hit 'pear like de plantation liv once mo', an de ain' no mo' scufflin', an' de ole times done come back ag'in, an' I heah meh kerridge-horses stompin' in de stalls, an' de place all cleared up ag'in, an' fence all roun' de pahsture, an' I smell de wet clover-blossoms right good, an' Marse Phil an' Meh Lady done come back, an' runnin' all roun' me, climbin' up on meh knees, callin' me 'Unc' Billy,' an pesterin' me to go fishin', while somehow Meh Lady an' de Cun'l, settin' dyah on de steps wid dee voice hummin' low like water runnin' in de' dark—(I, 166-67).

The wedding of the Northern man and Southern lady takes place in the Southern mansion before the pictures of Marse Phil and his mother: the Southern past is thus kept directly before us, a legacy that will be inherited by these lovers. Page writes what he considers to be a story of reconciliation, but it is a story in which the characters are reconciled to the Southern way of life. So insistent is the author on emphasizing the strength of Southern traditions that he finds it necessary to give the children of Captain Wilton and Meh Lady not the characteristics of their father—he is only partially Southern—but of their dead uncle, who is their link with all that was noble in plantation times!

"An' dat Phil, suh," he broke off, rising from the ground on which we had been seated for some time, "dat Phil, suh, he mo' like Marse Phil 'n he like he pa; an' Billy—he ain' so ole, but he ain' fur behine him."

"Billy," I said; "he's named after—"

"Go 'way, Marster," he said deprecatingly, "who gwine name gent'man after a ole nigger?" (I, 167)

IV "Ole 'Stracted": The Derangement of Loyalty

In "Ole 'Stracted," Page wrote one of his finest stories and one of the most poignant tales in the fiction of the local-color movement. He uses his own idiom now, and he tells the simple story of a Negro slave who has been sold to someone other than his master; the slave's "wife and boy [have] been sold to some other person at the same time for twelve hundred dollars." The Negro, Ole 'Stracted, claims that "his master [is] coming in the summer to buy him back and take him home, and [will] bring him his wife and child when he [comes]" (I, 186). This modest idea, that seems to threaten the reader with sentimentality, is firmly controlled by Page: he presents his central character as "'stracted," as a deranged old man whose obsession takes on credibility because of his mental condition. The story is about the derangement of loyalty, the utter inability of the slave to adjust himself to a Reconstruction period in which his master does not guide and protect him. One may dispute the historical validity of the author's creation, one may accuse him of perpetuating the notion of Negro infantilism, but there is a fictional validity that transcends the real world: the Negro's loneliness and nostalgia and loss and ultimate madness are thoroughly convincing, especially as seen by the white narrator and the other Negroes in the story.

In post-bellum times Ole 'Stracted has no identity because there is no identifiable world that he knows: he waits for his Master to tell him his name—"*He* know it—got it set down in de book" (I, 190)—and until that time he is unrelated to any real time or place. His entrance into this new, bewildering world as a nameless orphan is macabre and grotesque, like that of the Kafkaesque hero: "His advent in the neighborhood had been mysterious. The first that was known of him was one summer morning, when he was found sitting on the bench beside the door of this cabin, which had long been unoccupied and left to decay" (I, 186). Everything since the day he was sold has been "a blank to him, and as he could not tell the name of his master or wife, or even his own name, and as no one was left old enough to remember him, the neighborhood having been entirely deserted after the war, he simply passed as a harmless old lunatic laboring under a delusion" (I, 186).

But his insanity is not totally certain—like Hawthorne, Page enhances credibility by casting his own doubt on preposterous events and people. Furthermore, the old man has a self-perception not usually associated with derangement; he violently denounces a Negro woman when she calls him Ole 'Stracted—" 'dat ain' my name,' answered the old man, promptly. It was the first time he had ever disowned the name" (I, 190). Page gives his nameless hero a tragic dimension by making him clearly aware of his condition; Ole 'Stracted is a victim of the Civil War and Reconstruction, and Page wants the reader to see him as a martyr to his race. "Their [the other Negroes'] eyes were now accustomed to the darkness, and they saw that the only article of furniture which the room contained was the wretched bed or bench on which the old man was stretched. The light sifting through the chinks in the roof enabled them to see his face, and that it had changed much in the last twenty-four hours, and an instinct told them that he was near the end of his long waiting" (I, 190).

Ole 'Stracted's death is presented in all its pathos. The author has discovered here the perfect perspective for his story. By evoking through a final delirium the great longing of this man for the only master he has known, by establishing the Negro's sorrow through hallucinatory gestures that come moments before his death, Page projects the tragedy of the post-Civil War South in compelling terms:

"It's all in dyah . . . twelve hundred dollars . . . I wucked night an' day forty year to save dat money for marster; you know dee teck all he land an' all he niggers an' tu'n him out in de old fiel'? I put 'tin dyah 'ginst he come. You ain't know he comin' dis evenin', is you? Heah, help me on wid dat shut, gal—I stan'in' heah talkin' an' maybe ole marster waitin'. Push de do' open so you kin see. Forty year ago," he murmured, as Polly jambed the door back and returned to his side—"forty year ago dee come an' levelled on me: marster sutny did cry. 'Nem min',' he said,

'I comin' right down in de summer to buy you back an' bring
you home.' He's comin', too—nuver tol' me a lie in he life—comin'
dis evenin'. Make 'aste. . . . Oon marster be glad to see me? . . .
You known we growed up togerr? I been waitin' so long I feared
dee 'mos' done forgit me. You reckon dee is? . . . Heish! you
heah dat! . . . Gord! I knowed it . . . Dyah dee come. Now watch
'em smile . . ."

The evening sun, dropping on the instant to his setting,
flooded the room with light; but as Ephraim gently eased him
down and drew his arms from around him, it was the light of
the unending morning that was on his face. His Master had at
last come for him, and after his long waiting, Ole 'Stracted had
indeed gone home. (I, 192, 193, 194, 195)

V *"No Haid Pawn" and "Polly: A Christmas Recollection"*

"No Haid Pawn" is the one story in *In Ole Virginia* that does
not emphasize the historical significance of the vanished Southern past. It pretends to be no more than a ghost story—complete with haunted house and ghost, a man "of gigantic stature
and superhuman strength [who has] possessed appetites and
vices in proportion to his size," one who has "preserved his
wonderful strength by drinking human blood" (I, 207). The
story, in its emphasis on the macabre and grotesque, resembles
the supernatural tales of Edgar Allan Poe, a fellow Virginian
whom Page admired. Page is successful in creating the sense
of terror that he felt as a boy when he was shut up in this same
house; that night he remembered all the legends associated
with the house and in the middle of the night "heard the door
pushed wide open" and was certain that "the murderer of No
Haid Pawn had left his grave, and that his ghost was coming
up that stair." The house burns down, and "the spot with all
its secrets [lies] buried under its dark waters" (I, 227). The
reader is left with an impression of superstitious boys before
the war who live in a quiet rural community and, like Tom
Sawyer, eagerly seek adventure; as such, "No Haid Pawn" is "a
vivid story of the supernatural."[24]

The last tale in *In Ole Virginia*—"Polly: A Christmas Revelation"—returns to the themes of Page's other fiction concerning
the ante-bellum plantation life. Again it is a child's world
before the Civil War, which is almost tantamount to saying it

is an innocent, prelapsarian world before the Fall; again it is young love thwarted by political conflict and finally reconciled in a traditionally sentimental fashion. The story needs only brief comment, for it is the thinnest of these early tales about the pre-war South. Polly—"the tenderest little thing in the world"—is prevented from marrying her neighbor Bob because of her uncle's objections. The objections are political: the Colonel, Polly's uncle, is a staunch Whig, a conservative who denounces in flamboyant Southern rhetoric all those who challenge his slightest prejudice; Bob, who has prepared himself as a lawyer, leads the Locofoco party. Both men are loyal Southerners, Page reminds us, but Bob clearly represents the finest qualities of the South and suggests its future. Throughout Page's work, the Whigs represent the antagonists, and in some cases—in *Red Rock* particularly—they resort to a brutality that the author condemns. An important characteristic of Page is that "virtually all the characters of [his] fiction who, on the eve of the Civil War, might be considered spokesmen for the author's own point of view, were conservatives who urged moderation, and hesitated to resort to a policy of secession."[25]

But in "Polly: A Christmas Revelation" politics are only a vaguely suggested background to an excessively maudlin story. The political differences between the Colonel and Bob are an unconvincing reason for the lovers' separation, and the Colonel's adamant attitude is irritating and almost psychotic in its unwarranted hysteria. His niece, like a faithful heiress of sentimental fiction, obeys him and rejects her lover; but when the Colonel opposes Bob beyond reason—even beyond the reason of Polly—the lovers elope and marry. Finally they return so that the Colonel can heed his niece's imprecations and accept his political foe into his family.

The story is obviously banal; what commands the reader's attention are two caricatures: one of a Negro, Torm Drinkwater, who is forever drunk—Page is successful with his Negro types, although his sympathy is often tainted by irritating condescension—and one of the uncle, who, although extremely drawn, represents Page's image of the secessionist. The uncle, the author's Southern version of Sir Roger de Coverley, was based on Addison's character;[26] he is a conservative, a rhetorician, a dandy (he takes an hour to dress himself), a "gentleman"—and an unyielding bigot.

VI   In Ole Virginia

These stories, collected in 1887 under the title *In Ole Virginia,* represent the author's lasting contribution to American literature. Like most local colorists, Page describes a small area and a short period of time; he cannot develop beyond a close description of what he has seen and heard, and he possesses "so little inventive genius" that he needs "in almost every case to draw upon an incident or a character from real life."[27] *In Ole Virginia* acquaints the reader with the world of Thomas Nelson Page; later volumes, like *On Newfound River* (1890) and *Bred in the Bone* (1904), explore other aspects of that world, but the major themes are formulated and fully realized in this first published work. Creatively, he does not develop beyond the excellence of his early tales. Whenever he departs from his closed world before the war, as in *Gordon Keith* and *John Marvel, Assistant,* he is not successful—and his fiction can hardly be distinguished from most sentimental literature of the period.

But in "Marse Chan," "Unc' Edinburg's Drowndin'," "Meh Lady," and "Ole 'Stracted," he re-creates a dead civilization and generates it with mythical qualities. Writing late in the nineteenth century, he draws upon attitudes of earlier Southern writers and distills them into a fiction that is idealized. Heroism is a vital, necessary force, and it is the premise upon which all of Page's work is based. It leads inevitably to an idyllic past in which idealization is possible because the people themselves believed in a code of heroism. One can find other manifestations of this code in nineteenth-century Southern life as well as literature. William Gilmore Simms, for example, told a Northern traveler in 1866 that "South Carolina, sir, was the flower of modern civilization. Our people were the most hospitable, the most accomplished, having the highest degree of culture and the highest sense of honor, of any people, I will not say of America, sir, but of any country on the globe."[28]

But Page, more than any other Southern writer in the nineteenth century, fixes the various qualities of the code—honor, loyalty, courtesy, hospitality, sectional chauvinism—and motivates his characters according to these abstract attitudes. What gives *his* fiction a special poignance is the sense that this way of life has surrendered to another; he was "among the first to see that the old life was passing away; and he wisely avoided describing the great battles of the war and instead pictured the changes in the social life which were brought on by war and reconstruction."[29] Page, writing when realism was to make his attitude seem even more sentimental and old-fashioned than it was, assumed the role of a literary attorney who defended the South to the nation: "The South had no chronicler," observed a sympathetic Southern critic at the turn of the century, and "found itself arraigned at the bar of the world without . . . defense."[30]

Page was completely successful as propagandist, for only a year after the publication of *In Ole Virginia,* Albion W. Tourgée —Radical Republican and author of *A Fool's Errand* (1879)—was able to say that "not only is the epoch of the war the favorite field of American fiction today, but the Confederate soldier is the popular hero. Our literature has become not only Southern in type but distinctly Confederate in sympathy."[31]

The point of view that is governed by a belief in the possibilities of heroism is no longer fashionable—contemporary writers have said "a farewell to arms"; and, since Hemingway and Fitzgerald, most authors have concerned themselves with subjects that have been distinctly anti-heroic. This was not so true of many American authors in the nineteenth century—Emerson, Whitman, Twain, and Crane believed at least in the possibility of heroism—and certainly was not true of sentimental writers like Page. If one wants to understand nineteenth-century Southern fiction, if one cares to witness the code by which so many authors measured the morality of their characters, Page is a sensible beginning. And the beginning—the thematic center —of Page's body of work is most clearly and eloquently stated in the memorable stories of *In Ole Virginia.*

CHAPTER 2

The Old South

IN THE YEARS from 1883 through 1893 Page practiced law in Richmond, Virginia. After the appearance of "Old 'Stracted" in *Harper's New Monthly Magazine* in October, 1886, he did not publish again until May, 1888, when *Two Little Confederates* appeared serially in the *St. Nicholas Magazine;* but he delivered numerous lectures on Southern life before the war. Page did not feel a great urgency to write, in spite of the success of his early stories. In a revealing letter to his future mother-in-law, written January 25, 1886, when he was in the midst of creating his finest stories, he assured her that he was a responsible young lawyer but did not begin to suggest his hopes as a future author: "I have endeavored to let Miss Annie [his fiancée] know from the beginning that I was dependent on my profession for my living and that we should have to live very modestly; but I hope to keep her comfortable, and my Practice while not a lucrative one is a fair one, and its steady growth, I think, justifies me in the hope that steadiness industry and perseverance will enable me to do so."[1]

Page had practical, immediate concerns at this time. Besides his law practice, which he continued in a partnership with his cousin, Thomas Nelson Carter, until his retirement in 1893, he had invested in land, hoping to make a fortune from iron ore deposits in western Virginia; but the land property did not make him rich, and the four-year experience found its only usefulness in a short section of a later novel, *Gordon Keith* (1903). Of still greater concern was the love he had for Anne Seddon Bruce, whom he had met in 1885. She was the seventeen-year-old sister of a neighbor and was to be the prototype of those innumerable young Southern belles who recur throughout his fiction. She wore "blue satin and an ostrich fan" when they first met; she had an impressive pedigree; she was a paradigm of good manners; and, according to Page, she was his model and his inspiration.² With only the slightest literary flourish she became Miss Charlottle in "Unc' Edinburg's Drowndin'" and other idealizations. They married on July 28, 1886, and traveled for their honeymoon to Europe, returning to Richmond ´in the autumn. But their happiness was short-lived, for in December, 1888, she died at the age of twenty of a throat hemorrhage.

The experience was traumatic for Page, and in his extreme melancholy he turned to Catholicism, attracted by the absolute quality of church dogma; but he never converted and slowly his grief abated. In 1890, after a trip abroad, he began to lecture in various sections of the South, speaking of the manners and mores of the old South and reading from *In Ole Virginia*. These lectures were highly successful—Page seems to have been a genial, ingratiating speaker³—and helped to increase his popularity. At Vanderbilt University he was acknowledged as a spokesman of the old South by Professor William Malone Baskervill, the famous scholar of Southern literature and life. He read in Georgia and Texas and then turned to the North, where audiences were also sympathetic. In Boston, New York, and Chicago, he told his listeners how life was before the war, sometimes sharing the platform with his friend and fellow author, F. Hopkinson Smith. On a lecture tour in Chicago, Page met Mrs. Florence Lathrop Field, a young, wealthy widow who was the sister-in-law of Marshall Field. They married on June 6, 1893, and settled in Washington, D.C., thus ending a period in his life that would now be recollected only in fiction. From this time until his death in 1922, he was to lead a cosmopolitan, sophisticated life that had little to do with the provincial world of his stories.

As a consequence of his many lectures, Page became well known as a literary spokesman, at times as a literary apologist, of the South. His impressionistic essays, which range from literary history in "Literature in the South Before the War" and a view of Southern customs in "Social Life in Old Virginia Before the War" to a description of Negro inferiority in "The Race Question," gave an intellectual weight to the dramatic, emotional evocation of ante-bellum times in his fiction. These essays are like the acts of a dutiful and loving son; in them he records the culture, the manners, morals, and customs of the South that he

had suggested in his early stories. He tries "to be directly serviceable and, in a more distinct sense than elsewhere, his aim [is]
practical rather than artistic, informative rather than merely
literary."[4] These writings were published in 1892 in *The Old
South: Essays Social and Political;* they make clear, in a defini-
tive way, the premises of all the author's writings on the South.

I The Old South

In 1889 Page published "Literature in the South Before the
War," in which he calls the roll of ante-bellum Southern authors,
those who established the tradition upon which he built his own
fictional world. John Pendleton Kennedy, William Gilmore
Simms, John Esten Cooke, and other writers form a school of
writing that he realizes is popularly romantic. He notes the great
dependence on Scott's fiction, and he offers judicious and tem-
perate estimates of their work.[5] His detachment is noteworthy—
there is little attempt to give the literature a dimension it does
not have; and he turns his attention to the reasons for the absence of first-rate talent and genuine literary activity in this
period. He observes that before the war there was a practical
interest in agriculture, an absence of large cities (where culture
usually thrives), much political activity, and the great concern
over slavery. These conditions, he rightly suggests, caused the
South to have a very small reading audience, a discouragment to
potential artists.

In a second article, "Literature in the South Since the War"
(1891), Page is also judicious in his view of the Southern
literary scene. He lists dozens of post-bellum Southern authors
but does not measure their achievement too closely. He warns
the reader that "it is not the purpose of this paper to discuss
critically the literary work which has been produced by the
South since the war, but rather to indicate what has been
effected and to explain its genesis." Page recognizes Cable,
Harris, and Mary Murfree as important local colorists and notes
that the South should become the subject for great literature.
"Upon a survey of the conditions which at present exist, it appears to the writer that the South now presents a field for literature such as cannot be elsewhere found.[6]

Other essays collected in *The Old South* deal more with the
social life of old Virginia and tend to be chauvinistic; they read

as if Page has assumed responsibility for the defense of Southern and, more specifically, Virginian history. In essays like "Glimpses of Life in Colonial Virginia" and "Colonial Life," he establishes the background out of which grew the recollections of heroic behavior that appear in "Marse Chan" and "Meh Lady":

> Whatever the faults of the Virginians were they were the faults of a virile and independent race. Their virtues and their vices were those of the corresponding English classes from which they came, modified by the conditions which surrounded them in the new country. Every planter was to some extent a captain— a ruler over things few or many; but yet a ruler. And the qualities developed were those of a ruling class. But there was a class which existed far below this ruler class also with virile traits and clear-cut character. It was not dependence; for they were in their poverty as independent as their wealthier neighbors. Slavery had not, as has so often been insisted, destroyed the dignity of labor, so much as it had furnished the laborers to perform most of the work. Thus, there was not the call for labor that existed in countries where the laborers were all free. Those who in other countries or sections composed the laboring class in the South were known as "poor whites," but however poor they were they retained their personal independence. They despised all menial employment and lived much as their ancestors had lived. Poor but independent, they exhibited the traits of frontiersmen, lovers of the woods; fond of fishing and hunting, and often skilled woodsmen; hospitable and kindly, pleasant in manner, firm in friendship, and fierce in enmity; ready to follow the lead of the upper class; but stout in their opinions when formed, and tenacious of their rights. (XIII, 151-52)

Such passages are interspersed between sections that deal with the more prosaic subject of taxes—which were levied only by the Virginia Assembly—or Virginia manners, which were an extension of English country life; and these passages are patently chauvinistic and defensive. When, for example, one English commentator on early life in Virginia, the Reverend Andrew Burnaby, claims that the Virginians whom he saw lacked enterprise, Page of course disagrees; but his evidence seems to be simply the authority of his own character. And, when Burnaby goes on to state that Virginian women "are seldom accomplished" and are "immoderately fond of dancing," Page suggests that the society the author visited was not the most representative or the best.

He is justified in modifying some of these commentaries by English travelers, for many of them were unfairly condescending and contemptuous. But it is equally true that the barren culture, the rural provinciality to which they allude, was present; and Page's attempts to justify it are unconvincing and excessive.

The aspects of ante-bellum Southern culture that were unique are carefully and lovingly described in an extremely important essay, "Social Life in Old Virginia Before the War." No single piece offers a clearer index to Page's mind and, by extension, to the Southern mind; it presents, in a self-conscious, affectionate way, the types of people and their various customs that the author assumes as the background of *In Ole Virginia*. The essay, as Page confesses, is indebted to Dr. George W. Bagby's *The Old Virginia Gentleman,* a series of sketches on Virginian life before the Civil War. He calls Bagby's sentimental book the "best sketch yet written in the South," and of course the reason is that it is conveyed in Page's own manner by "one who knew and loved Virginia well" (XII, 176).

Page describes the various ante-bellum types and their characteristics, writing first of the Southern lady. She was indeed a remarkable woman, for she was a "mistress, manager, doctor, nurse, counsellor, seamstress, teacher, housekeeper, slave, all at once. She was at the beck and call of every one, especially of her husband, to whom she was 'guide, philosopher, and friend' " (XII, 185). This lady, familiar to the reader in "Meh Lady," is idealized to the point that she takes on divine, mystical traits: "What she was only her husband knew, and even he stood before her in dumb, half-amazed admiration, as he might before the inscrutable vision of a superior being. What she really was, was known only to God. Her life was one long act of devotion—devotion to God, devotion to her husband, devotion to her children, devotion to her servants, to her friends, to the poor, to all humanity" (XII, 185-86).

The Southern gentleman, the master of the plantation, was more self-conscious about his own superiority—and that superiority, the author makes clear, depended on his pedigree and race. The Southern gentleman carried on the noblest characteristics of the Anglo-Saxon race:

He was proud, but never haughty to dishonor. To that he was inexorable. He believed in God, he believed in his wife, he believed in his blood. He was chivalrous, he was generous, he was

usually incapable of fear or meanness. To be a Virginia gentleman was the first duty; it embraced being a Christian and all
virtues. He lived as one; he left it as a heritage to his children.
He was fully appreciative of both of the honors and the responsibilities of his position. He believed in a democracy, but
understood that the absence of a titled aristocracy had to be
supplied by a class more virtuous than he believed them to be.
This class was, of course, that to which he belonged.[7]

Page characterizes the Southerner as "a wonderful talker,"
hospitable, an "exponent of that grave and knightly courtesy
which under all conditions has become associated with the title
'Virginia gentleman'" (XII, 192). The other roles that he gives
to people on the plantation are equally romantic; the gentle
Negro mammy, the severe butler, the kindly driver, all take
their positions behind the Southern gentleman and lady and
contribute to a social life that "was one of singular sweetness and
freedom from vice," which "asked nothing more than to be let
alone" (XII, 200). He apologizes for his treatment of old
Virginia, admitting that he is "painfully aware of the inadequacy
of [his] picture. But who could do justice to the truth!" (XII,
205). In fact, he has left no room for human differences; the
"truth" he would do justice to is already an idealization of his
mind, an impossible vision, a distorted recrudescence of the way
life *might have been* in old Virginia. As Jay B. Hubbell points
out, the kind of life that Page depicts is part of a

> Southern literary legend which pictures a Golden Age in the
> slaveholding South. Now the remarkable thing about this legend
> is that apart from the poor-whites it plays up the very same
> classes as the Northern legend: the great planters and the Negro
> slaves. Like the Northern legend, it practically ignores some
> four million yeomen farmers. They did not belong to the First
> Families. . . . In Virginia in 1860 in a population of over one
> million whites there were only 52,128 men who owned any
> slaves. There were only 114 who owned as many as one hundred.
> At least nineteen out of every twenty slaveholders was a yeoman,
> who held two or three slaves and worked in the tobacco fields
> beside them. The great planters were few in numbers, but it
> was from their class that as a rule the people chose their
> representatives in Congress and the General Assembly.[8]

Put beside these sober facts, Page's account of life in old
Virginia is an unreliable, sentimental gesture; indeed, the end of

his essay, mellow with memories, rises to the lyrical level of a
requiem, and as such is beyond analysis:

> It [the Old South] largely contributed to produce this nation; it
> led its armies and its navies; it established this government so
> firmly that not even it could overthrow it; it opened up the great
> West; it added Louisiana and Texas, and more than trebled our
> territory; it Christianized the negro race in a little over two
> centuries, impressed upon it regard for order, and gave it the
> only civilization it has ever possessed since the dawn of history.
> It has maintained the supremacy of the Caucasian race, upon
> which all civilization seems now to depend. It produced a
> people whose heroic fight against the forces of the world has
> enriched the annals of the human race—a people whose fortitude
> in defeat has been even more splendid than their valor in war.
> It made men noble, gentle, and brave, and women tender and
> pure and true. It may have fallen short in material development
> in its narrower sense, but it abounded in spiritual development; it
> made the domestic virtues as common as light and air, and filled
> homes with purity and peace.
>
> It has passed from the earth, but it has left its benignant in-
> fluence behind it to sweeten and sustain its children. The ivory
> palaces have been destroyed, but myrrh, aloes, and cassia still
> breathe amid their dismantled ruins. (XII, 221)

Such an attitude, fostered and nourished by stories Page had
heard when he was a boy, suggests why he brings a stock, sentimental approach to subjects of the Civil War and the Reconstruction. No matter how concerned he may be with the present action of the war itself, no matter how horrified he may be with
the desecration that attends Reconstruction, the old South broods
behind the action, evoking the memory of the way life used to
be—Page can always return in fantasy to that Edenic time.

In two brief essays he continues his survey and record of
colonial Virginia. "The Old Virginia Lawyer" describes the
typical man who held the first position of the community, who
felt no need for books and was in fact anti-intellectual. But,
according to Page, he was a "gladiator in court," a very serious
man who was devoted to his client. Once again the reader feels
himself confronted with a vast social drama in which the lawyer
takes his part. More urgent, because it is more personal, is the
short "Two Colonial Places," in which the author speaks of his
forebears and the establishment of his own plantation home,

Rosewell. He traces the history of his maternal family, the Nelsons, and boasts of Thomas Nelson, the founder of Yorktown, and of his grandson Governor Thomas Nelson, who was a signer of the Declaration of Independence. This branch of his family was left poor. The Pages, however, established the largest mansion in 1725; there was a local legend, too, that Thomas Jefferson wrote and showed the Declaration of Independence to John Page in that manorial house. As the author describes the mansion, it comes to incarnate that element in the South which helped to found the nation and which later symbolizes the solid traditions of the old South.

Part of the reason for Page's chauvinism and elaborate defense of the South is his conviction that the Southern people have never been fairly represented in history:

> There is no true history of the South. In a few years there will be no South to demand a history. What of our history is known by the world to-day? What is our position in history? How are we regarded? Nothing or next to nothing is known of our true history by the world at large. By a limited class in England there is a vague belief founded on a sentiment that the South was the aristocratic section of this country, and that it stood for its rights, even with an indefensible cause. By a somewhat more extended class its heroism is admired sufficiently to partly condone its heresies. But these are a small part of the public. By the world at large we are held to have been an ignorant, illiterate, cruel, semi-barbarous section of the American people, sunk in brutality and vice, who have contributed nothing to the advancement of mankind: a race of slave-drivers, who, to perpetuate human slavery, conspired to destroy the Union, and plunged the country into war. Of this war, precipitated by ourselves, two salient facts are known—that in it we were whipped, and that we treated our prisoners with barbarity. (XII, 346)

Page, like so many other Southern authors before and during his time, has taken it upon himself to champion the South; and his political as well as literary role often causes him to become too obviously tendentious. He feels with some justification that the South's "every act was misjudged, her every word misinterpreted," largely because "the South has left the writing of her civilization to the North" (XII, 360). He is also justified when he calls attention to the great importance of the historian's role in resolving or aggravating sectional differ-

ences. But his advice to the future Southern historian suggests
an extreme position that would only distort history. The historian,
he maintains, ought to revere "the greatness of [his] past" and to
maintain "a pride of race." These are the "two cardinal elements"
that "made the Greek; they made the Saxon; they made the
Southerner." This historian should remember that

> whatever else may be said, of this much are we sure, that the
> South and its civilization produced a race of soldiers which
> has never been surpassed. . . . He must have the sagacity to
> detect whatever of evil existed in the civilization he shall
> chronicle, though it be gleaming with the gilding of romance; he
> must have the fortitude to resist all temptation to deflect by so
> much as a hair's breadth from the absolute and the inexorable
> facts, even if an angel should attempt to beguile him. He must
> know and tell the truth, the whole truth, and nothing but the
> truth, so help him, God! (XII, 364, 369)

That truth, one is forced to conclude, is too often Page's and not
an objective, disinterested truth. His memories of the old régime,
as Jay B. Hubbell notes, are "so idealized that he cannot see it
in any other way even when he assumes the role of historian."[9]

The distorted mirror through which Page looks at Southern
problems is most obviously present whenever he writes of the
Negro—and especially of the insurgent Negro who insists upon
his legal rights. In a long and painfully executed essay, "The
Race Question," he outlines very clearly his view of race relations; his comments throw into bitter relief all of his attitudes
toward social customs in the old South and make the reader
aware of how absolutely committed he is toward the conservative political position.

The essay is an answer to those political and social commentators who had sought increased rights for the Negro, among
whom George Washington Cable was one of the most articulate
spokesmen. Cable had delivered a speech before the Massachusetts Club of Boston on February 22, 1890, in which he rejected
the Southern position on the race question and went on to say
that "The Problem is whether American citizens shall not enjoy
equal rights in the choice of their rulers. It is not a question of
the Negro's right to rule. *It is simply a question of their right to
choose rulers; and as in reconstruction days they selected more*

white men for office than men of their own race, they would probably do so now."[10]

Page, in rebuttal to Cable and all those who sympathize with his attitudes, intends to demonstrate that the question is not "merely whether the Negro shall or shall not have the right to choose his ruler, but is a great race question on which depends the future as well as the present salvation of the nation" (219). What one reads in the pages that follow, however, is the author's attempted solution for the salvation of the South. Throughout the essay he is intent upon establishing the racial differences between the white Anglo-Saxon and the African Negro, newly migrated to America. And the burden of meaning is that the master-slave relationship was not so immoral or so impractical as hostile observers have claimed—in fact, a partial regression to that relationship would be entirely proper. Before Page offers any solution to a problem that has become so complex and threatening to him, he reiterates in the most elaborate way his position of racial supremacy. It is difficult to think of another essay in American literature, written by a serious and responsible author, that marshals the sundry arguments for Negro inferiority in a more comprehensive way:

> What of value to the human race has the Negro mind as yet produced? In art, in mechanical development, in literature, in mental and moral science, in all the range of mental action, no notable work has up to this time come from a Negro.
>
> In the earliest records of the human race, the monuments of Egypt and Syria, he is depicted as a slave bearing burdens; after tens of centuries he is still a menial. Four thousand years have not served to whiten the pigments of the frame, nor developed the forces of the intellect. The leopard cannot change his spots to-day, nor the Ethiopian his skin, any more than they could in the days of Jeremiah the son of Hilkiah. . . . Where the Negro has thriven it has invariably been under the influence of the stronger race. Where these have been wanting, whatever other conditions have existed, he has sensibly and invariably reverted toward the original type. Liberia, Hayti, Congo, are all in one line. (249-51)

.   .   .   .

> But suppose that the statements of others, whose observation has enabled them to pick out a well-to-do [Negro] lawyer or dentist or doctor or restauranteur, be different, it only proves that in individual instances they may rise to a fair level; it simply

emphasizes the fact that these are exceptions to the great rule, and does not in the least affect the argument, which is that the Negroes *as a race* have never exhibited much capacity to advance; that as a race they are inferior to other races. (257)

. . . .

They are barbers and white-washers, shoe-blacks and chimney-sweeps. Here and there we find a lawyer or two, unhappily with their practice in inverse ratio to their principle. Or now and then there is a doctor. But almost invariably these are men with a considerable infusion of white blood in their veins. And even they have, in no single instance, attained a position which in a white would be deemed above mediocrity. Fifteen years ago there were in Richmond a number of Negro tobacco and other manufacturers in a small way. Now there are hardly any except undertakers.

They do not appear to possess the faculties which are essential to conduct any business in which reason has to be applied beyond the immediate act in hand.

They appear to lack the faculty of organization on which rests all successful business enterprise.

They have been losing ground as mechanics. . . . Where they have been brought into contact with the stronger race under conditions in which they derive aid, as in cities, they have in certain directions improved; where they have lacked this stimulating influence, as in sections of the country where the association has steadily diminished, they have failed to advance. (278, 279)

. . . .

One of these principles [the writer holds after having studied the race problem] is the absolute and unchangeable superiority of the white race—a superiority, it appears to him, not due to any mere adventitious circumstances, such as superior educational and other advantages during some centuries, but an inherent and essential superiority, based on superior intellect, virtue, and constancy. He does not believe that the Negro is the equal of the white, or ever could be the equal. Race superiority is founded on courage (or, perhaps, "constancy" is the better word), intellect, and the domestic virtues, and in these the white is the superior of every race. (292-93)

In the midst of this full-scale indictment Page's reassurance that he has great affection for the Negro seems bitterly ironic: "What has been stated has been said in no feeling of personal hostility, or even unfriendliness to the Negro, for I have no un-friendliness toward any Negro on earth; on the contrary, I have a feeling of real friendliness toward many of that race, and am the well-wisher of the whole people" (262). Still, as automatic as this attitude appears, as condescending as it is after the invidious judgments he has made of the Negro, it is true to a degree; one cannot help but feel his deep affection for the "old-time" Negro—the ante-bellum Negro—throughout his fiction and essays. But of course this retrogressive attitude does not mitigate his views in 1892, when "The Race Question" was first published; he remains as one of the leading literary reactionaries of the period, unwilling to note the extreme economic and social deprivation of the Negro. Page's bitterness grew out of his realization that a new generation of Negroes was reaching maturity who insisted upon equality; and he was incapable of considering the Negro as an "entity apart from the white man."[11] It is wrong to think that the Negroes in Page's fiction are only faithful and content. This type of Negro is simply best known because he appears in Page's best fiction; but unattractive portraits of insurgent, vulgar Negroes appear throughout his work in the *Pastime Stories*, for example, and in other tales like "P'laski's Recognition." "In *Red Rock* there are as many instances of ludicrous stupidity and presumption on the part of the Negroes as of their loyal and intelligent behavior."[12]

Page's racism leads to the only conceivable solution for him— education. "Education is now the talisman,"[13] he asserts, and he falls in line with most other nineteenth-century commentators on the race question. Albion W. Tourgée in *An Appeal to Caesar*, George Washington Cable in *The Silent South*, R. C. Winthrop, C. F. Adams—all these writers and political leaders, so different in their various attitudes toward the Negro, realize that only through education will the problem be ameliorated. But Page is not nearly so specific as his contemporaries; his suggestions as to the form of this education appear in the last few pages of his essay and are too vague to be of service. Basically, he wants "the Negroes to divide up into classes, with character and right conduct as the standard for elevation. When they make distinctions themselves, others will recognize their distinctions" (307). The Negro, he feels, "must be taught the great elementary truths of morality and duty. Until he is so established in these that he claims to be on this ground the equal of the white, he can never be his equal on any other ground. When he is the equal of the white, it will make itself known. Until then, he is fighting not the white race, but a law of nature, universal and inexorable—that races rise or fall according to their character" (310).

In terms of race relations generally, his solution is traditional and conservative. He feels that "those outside of the South, who, most cocksure of their position where they were most in error, have tried to force a solution on lines contrary to natural and unchangeable laws" (293). And he rehearses the evils of Reconstruction and the corruption of carpetbaggers (forgetting that there were many Radical Republicans who came to the South for quite idealistic purposes). If "the Negro were simply let alone and left to his own resources," he concludes, "with such help as equity or philanthropy might contribute—in other words, if the whites and blacks were left to settle their difficulties and troubles in the various States and sections precisely as they would be left were all whites or all blacks," then these bitter problems would be solved (293-94). "Left alone, the whites and the blacks of the South would settle difficulties along the lines of substantial equity" (294). What Page wants, quite obviously, is a revival of the old relationship between Negro and white—one in which there is no question, on the practical level, of which is the superior race.

> We have in the past had experience of the Negro fairly well trained and in amity with the white, where he recognized the latter's superiority. We have the high authority of one of the leading Negro teachers and leaders, that the Negro yearns toward the white. This is strongly corroborated by the well-known fact that wherever the Negroes and the Southern whites are let alone, and are not affected by outside influences, they, for the most part, live in harmony. If we keep on and manage the race question with firmness and with equity, we shall yet show the Negro that his true interest lies in maintaining amity with the Southern white. This we can never do if we take ground against educating him and leave the Northern white to advocate uplifting him. (300-1)

Page's demands were realized. As Rayford Logan has recently shown, Northern Republicans and Democrats deserted the Negro in the 1880's and 1890's. At the end of his administration, Hayes had left "white supremacy . . . more securely entrenched in the South" than when he had entered the White House; and

"Presidents Garfield, Arthur and Cleveland allowed the Southern question to simmer during the next eight years, 1881-1889." It had become evident by the end of Cleveland's first administration that "presidents of both parties uttered pious platitudes but said nothing and did nothing except to give a few jobs to professional Negro office-holders."[14] Though Page laments the era of Reconstruction and the new attitudes of many Negroes since the war, the fact is that the Radical Republicans ultimately suffered the notorious defeat of Reconstruction, and the South succeeded in establishing its point of view on the nation:

> For better or for worse Page, Harris, Allen, and their associates of the South, with the aid of Northern editors, critics, magazines, publishing houses, and theatres, had driven completely from the Northern mind the unfriendly picture of the South implanted there in the days of strife. In place of the discarded image they had fixed a far more friendly conception of a land basically American and loyal to the best traditions of the nation, where men and women had lived noble lives and had made heroic sacrifices to great ideals, where Negroes loved "de white folks," where magnolias and roses blossomed over hospitable homes that sheltered lovely maids and brave cadets, where romance of the past still lived, a land where, in short, the nostalgic Northerner could escape the wear and tear of expanding industry and growing cities and dwell in a Dixie of the storybooks which had become the Arcady of American tradition.[15]

In 1892, when "The Race Question" and the other essays included in *The Old South* were published, Page's career was at its peak. Now that Northerners had won the war and emancipated the Negro, they yearned for Southern stories and essays on the life they had destroyed; Page provided the stories in *In Ole Virginia* and the essays in *The Old South*. Seeking a simple solution to the race problem, Northerners disregarded Tourgée and Cable and heeded Page—they permitted the Negro problem to be a Southern problem. The image of Thomas Wentworth Higginson—"who as a youth had led a jail delivery of a recaptured fugitive slave, and who in the Civil War had commanded a regiment of Negro troops,—sitting in his study thirty years after the war had ended with a copy of 'Marse Chan' on his lap, shedding tears over the death of a slaveowner"[16] was typical of many other Northerners. "Our literature," as Tourgée wrote in 1888, "had become not only Southern in type, but distinctly Confederate in sympathy."[17]

II *Stories of the Civil War*

Page's four finest stories—"Marse Chan," "Unc' Edinburg's Drowndin'," "Meh Lady," and "Ole 'Stracted"—evoke that time "before the war" and achieve, in the words of F. P. Gaines, "a glamour, a mellow light, the like of which no author was able to command."[18] In a series of stories and sketches, which fall into that period from 1888-1894, Page writes more directly of the war itself and the way it affected the Southern people at home. He can never describe the conflict as intimately as other post-war authors like John W. De Forest (in *Miss Ravenel's Conversion from Secession to Loyalty*) or Albion W. Tourgée (in *Figs and Thistles*), and, wisely, he rarely tries. Page was only a child of eight when the Civil War began; his point of view is that of the outsider, and he offers the world of the sympathetic Southern wife or son or Negro servant who remained at home. But home in Oakland, Hanover County, Virginia, he reminds the reader, was very close to the battlefield —was, in a sense, a part of the battlefield itself.

His most elaborate recollection of experiences during the war is in *Two Little Confederates* (1888), a kind of Virginian Tom Sawyer without the relief of Mark Twain's humor. The story, written for children, romanticizes the war in stereotypical ways: the reader witnesses the Yankees who come to the Southern plantation to plunder the place; the mother of the two confederates who is the staunch and faithful Southern lady, and gives the boys a sense of stability in an otherwise insecure life; the Negroes who refuse to be lured away by the Yankees. One Yankee is kind to the confederate boy Frank; and, when the Yankee is dying of thirst, Frank comes to his aid, crying out, " 'I don't want him to die. I don't want him to die!' " (XI, 155). The soldier does die, however, and after the war his mother comes to this Virginia hinterland for her son's body. She is received hospitably by the Southern mother, who also feels that she has lost her own older son in battle. The mutual loss is poignant, although perhaps too obviously written to the formula of reconciliation; and the news of Southern defeat is impressive as it affects the women and boys at home. Emotions that normally are maudlin and banal are well-controlled here—there is little self-pity throughout the tale. But Page cannot restrain himself in the scene in which the father returns from the war: "It seemed like a funeral. The boys were near the steps, and their mother stood on the portico with her forehead resting against a pillar. No word was spoken. Into the yard they rode at a walk, and up to the porch. Then their father, who had not once looked up, put both his hands to his face, slipped from his horse, and walked up the steps, tears running down his cheeks, and took their mother into his arms. It *was* a funeral—the Confederacy was dead" (XI, 160).

Sentimental as this passage is, calculated as it is to make the reader weep, it still proves the fitting conclusion to a war tale as seen through the eyes of a Southern boy. Despair is the proper mood, and Page succeeds in evoking that mood as he does in the finest fiction of *In Ole Virginia*—the curtain falls at the end of an irrevocable tragedy. In *Two Little Confederates,* however, he mars his tale by pandering to the desire of his audience for a tale of reconciliation. He adds a happy ending, a contrived dénouement, in which the son of the Southern lady returns and marries his estranged lover. As Edmund Wilson points out, "It was hard to make the Civil War seem cosy, but Thomas Nelson Page did his best."[19]

Other stories, included in *Among the Camps; or Young People's Stories of the War* (1891), also show the war from the outsider's and the child's point of view; but they do not have the verisimilitude of *Two Little Confederates* and are merely anecdotal in nature. In "A Captured Santa Claus" (1888), the son of a Southern colonel helps his father gain an extended parole from the war; in "Kitty Kin and the Part She Played in the War" (1891), a cat halts warfare, for the moment, between the enemies—they pause to retrieve her from a tree; in "Nancy Pansy" (1889), a young girl reconciles North and South through her simple affection; in "Jack and Jake" (1891), owner and slave express their mutual love; in "Two Prisoners" (1892), a war widow suffers extreme loneliness. These stories are either frivolous or patently sentimental—they are written for children and are not intended to be serious; yet they have a brooding atmosphere of war hovering over them. The beginning of one chapter in "Nancy Pansy" begins: "In March, 186-, Middleburgh fell. That is, it fell into the hands of the Union army, and remained in their hands afterwards" (XI, 253). The ominous note struck here—and similar statements appear throughout these stories—frames the frivolity or banality of the characters; it gives normally sentimental behavior an unnatural and at times terrifying aspect and functions as a dark shadow that throws into relief the ephemeral brightness of the characters. These common experiences are an escape from war, from the reality that is everywhere behind the action of the stories.

III On Newfound River

On Newfound River (1891) explores, in a more explicit and comprehensive manner than do the stories of *In Ole Virginia*, the local color of rural old Virginia, the political tensions of the ante-bellum South, the varying positions on slavery, and, of course, the traditional attitudes of white masters toward their slaves. Furthermore, the narrative is replete with the typical sentimental devices that have become by this time Page's stock-in-trade: a love story whose conflict relies upon social distinctions; mistaken identity; the clash of a reactionary father and his more progressive liberal son. But the short novel is more than merely representative of Page's attitudes and more than an overt statement of those ideas implied in "Marse Chan" and "Meh Lady"; with all of its limitations, *On Newfound River* is one of the author's finest fictions. Written briskly but with care, it is leavened by amusing minor caricatures, by people who are molded and bound to the Southern landscape.

Page assumes an anti-literary pose, so common to this period, in a short preface which is really a warning to that reader who may discover a meaning beyond the sentimental incidents of the novel:

The reader will, perhaps, bear in mind that "On Newfound River" does not pretend to be a Novel; but is on its face a "Story,"— a Love-Story if you will—of simple Country Life in Old Virginia. The "setting" is wholly that of the Country, the surroundings are all those of a life far from cities, the incidents are, for the most part, those little commonplace events which might have taken place in a rural neighborhood before the war, where the gentry

ruled in a sort of manorial manner and their poorer neighbors
bore a relation to them part retainer, part friend.

In preparing a new edition for the press [the Plantation
Edition, published in 1906], the author has enlarged the work
by certain additions to the Story, with a view to making it more
complete and giving a somewhat fuller reflection of the life it
undertakes to mirror, somewhat as he did before with "The
Gentleman of the Black Stock." But no attempt has been made to
change it into a novel, or even to enlarge it beyond its original
scope. It was written as a Love-Story and a Love-Story, pure
and simple, it is. (III, Preface)

The defensive nature of this preface indicates that he was not
only aware that he had written a novel, as uneven as it may be,
but that his love story is burdened by many other elements—by
politics, most noticeably; by race relations, incidentally. The
finest single aspect of the book, as in all of his work, is the
local color: the quiet mood of the period, the description of
Virginia before the war. The war destroyed the eastern counties
of the state, where the Newfound River glides, but Page intends
to restore the area to literary posterity:

It lay right in the track of the armies, and the civilization which
existed there in the old days before the war has perished as
utterly as that of Nineveh or of Karnak. But at the time when
the events herein related occurred, the country on Newfound
was one of the old "neighborhoods" of the State. It was as retired
and as quiet as one of the coves of Newfound Millpond where
the water lilies slept in a repose undisturbed by the outside
current. Into this quiet life little excitement ever came from
the outer world with which the chief connecting link was the
sleepy mailrider who passed up the main road twice a week
dropping his papers at the "big-gates" which were the outward
signs of the plantations that lay secluded beyond the screening
woods and leaving his letters at the Crossroads post-office. The
excitement of that life was all supplied by the inhabitants themselves. Politics there meant how this or that or the other man
cast his vote; religion was gauged by the spiritual experiences
and conduct of this or that member, and civilization itself was
weighed and tested by the life lived on the plantations. But
even the events in their lives did not usually stir those denizens
more than the breezes stirred the lily pads which, though moved
a little on the surface, being anchored to the soil soon settled
back in their accustomed places. The Landons and others of

their kind ruled unquestioned in a sort of untitled manorial system; their poor neighbors stood in a peculiar relation to them, part friend, part retainer, the line between independence and vassalage being impalpable; and peace and plenty reigned over a smiling land. (III, 3-5)

The central conflict of *On Newfound River* involves Major Landon and an emigrant, Mr. Browne, who comes to this bucolic area with his granddaughter, Margaret Reid. Having bought a home from Major Landon, Browne settles in the community but does not join it; and he soon engenders the animosity of neighbors because of his inhospitality. Rumors about him soon spread among the people: "in time a word was whispered about concerning him which could only be whispered: 'Abolitionist'" (III, 10). But Page does not pursue any kind of bitter conflict here, nor does he develop Browne into so dangerous a character as an Abolitionist. Landon accuses Browne of letting his cows eat his corn, and Browne finally confesses guilt. So trivial a situation seems far too slight a prop on which to build a story, even a local-color story, but Page introduces a social distinction between Browne and Landon that makes the poaching humanly pathetic rather than dramatically artificial. And he strengthens this situation even more when the social differences of Landon and Browne are an obstacle to the young lovers of the novel; for, without very much surprise, the reader soon discovers that Margaret Reid, the granddaughter of Browne, and Bruce Landon, the son and heir of Major Landon's fortunes, are the lovers of the story.

Major Landon is an aristocratic planter whose family has had traditional wealth and prestige. When he discovers that his son has been carrying on a childhood romance with Browne's granddaughter, he denounces the boy: "I should think you'd be ashamed to associate with such people. They are low, and worthless, and unfit associates for a gentleman . . . they are nothing but common people" (III, 50). As an expression of his opposition, he sends the boy away to school for eight years; but, of course, the old man is unsuccessful in keeping the lovers apart—for love in Page's fiction knows neither the limitations of time or distance. When Bruce returns, he discovers a thoroughly realistic girl whose protracted innocence is credible because she has been a recluse, imprisoned by her grandfather and victim to his loneliness and crippled condition. Her education in Bruce's absence, given to her by her grandfather, has been traditional in nature: she has read the adventures of "Evelina, Clarissa Harlowe, Sir Charles Grandison, Pamela, Sir Roger de Coverley, Lord Orville, Lizzie Bennet, Mr. Darcy, Emma Woodhouse, and a few others besides the characters from the dramas of Corneille, Racine and Molière and other French classics" (II, 55). Her private life is less worldly, and she is ripe for Bruce's romantic overtures—although, of course, she does not accept him at first. When Page keeps the girl at a distance, suggesting her loneliness and frustration, he is effective and even intriguing; but, as he begins to describe the actual details of Margaret's life, he descends into sentimental obviousness, and the girl becomes the standard heroine of the popular novel.

Bruce Landon is that stock Southern hero the reader encounters in almost every work of Page; in *On Newfound River*, however, he is given more credible proportions as he comes into conflict with the poverty-stricken girl, and, more impressively, with his father. The very strong father-son relationship is Page's most successful attempt at such a description in his fiction. Since neither of them is threatened by a common political enemy, against which they would ordinarily join forces whatever their human differences, the novelist can explore their conflicts with some honesty. Out of their relationship grow all of the tensions of the novel:

> Bruce could not but admire the stern character of the old gentleman, who was inflexible in purpose, indomitable in will, and transparently honest in every word and act, however intolerant he might be and constitutionally incapable of yielding his opinion once formed on any subject. . . .
> Bruce found himself in a new life, almost wholly unknown to him. He had suddenly become the companion of the man who had always been to him the incarnation of pride and reserve. His father seemed not able to let him get out of his sight. If he went only to the stables, he invited him to come with him. He told him of all his affairs; talked over the politics of the country with him; consulted him; deferred to him. At the same time, he was treated like a distinguished guest. It was very new and very pleasant to him. The best wine was brought from the cellar: Madeira imported by his grandfather. The Major insisted on his riding his saddle-horse, and he himself rode another. No compliment could have been more marked and Bruce knew it. At last

the wide gap between them had been bridged and father and son found mutual delight in each other's presence; for in the new relation each avoided the subject [Bruce's love affair with Margaret Reid] where there might be a chance of difference. (III, 72, 76)

The Major urges his son to enter politics, and at this point the differences between the generations become most apparent. Bruce, who naturally gravitates toward the Democratic Party rather than the Whig, claims that "he could not hold with a party that created class distinctions, with a party that sponsored slavery." When he tells the Major that he thinks slavery is a sin, the father automatically responds: "Don't you go and fling away your bread and butter" (III, 103).

This young rebel soon discovers that he has more in common with his father than he thought, however, when he confronts his liberal lover, Margaret Reid, a girl whose opinions are original, provocative, and even threatening. She is dogmatic, the author tells the reader:

> . . . prompt in her judgment that "The Rape of the Lock" was a better poem than the "Essay on Man," and that "The Heart of Midlothian" was a finer novel than "Ivanhoe" and was prepared to back up her judgment with sundry sound reasons. . . . And when she touched on nearer and more practical matters, [Bruce Landon] was even more astonished. He had inherited most of his opinions as he had inherited his religion. He had accepted them without really thinking about them. To find a young girl questioning them and seriously thinking of the reasons for things which he had always assumed to be unquestionable astonished him and startled him somewhat. Hitherto he had never thought of a girl but as a beautiful thing to admire, to protect and to love; an ornament of life, a flower for a man to wear and enjoy. But here was some one who was wholly new to his experience. Here was intellect as well as beauty. (III, 187-88)

The crucial difference between the lovers, who represent the two sections of the traditional novel of reconciliation, is expressed in terms of slavery:

> Where could she have gotten her notion which she stated so simply that slavery was not a perpetual nor a divine institution and that it would some day be abolished and all the negroes be free! This was in direct variance with all the teaching Bruce

had ever received. Of course, he knew that there was a growing element in the North, who, now that they had gotten rid of their own slaves, wanted to take the slaves from the Southerners, but under that, as he had always heard, was sheer envy and, even there the great body of the people recognized the rights of the South. Did not the Bible teach slavery?—St. Paul and all of them?

"Well, if it did," said this serene-faced little philosopher, "it must have been only as a human institution which was allowed rather than inculcated. St. Paul had to take a good many things as he found them—and the great teaching of the church was for a new and moral life. The good God has told us to love Him with all our heart and soul and mind, and our neighbor as ourself, and this cannot be with slavery. You would not want any one to hold you in slavery?" (III, 188-89)

To dramatize the real political and social differences between this girl and Bruce, Page refers to *Uncle Tom's Cabin;* the young abolitionist girl has read it, but the Southern gentleman refuses to. "It is a travesty of Southern life," he asserts, "a jumble of libels on the South" (III, 191). This sudden Southern chauvinism seems indeed odd when Page has struggled to create a tension between father and son based fundamentally on the son's liberalism. The most suitable explanation, perhaps, is that the native values and traditions of Bruce Landon are far firmer and more significant than his attachment to Margaret Reid or his filial rebellion against his father. In any case, the inconsistent motivation is awkwardly apparent—it is as if Page were terrified at having any Southern gentleman renounce his heritage, and he quickly makes the son's rebellion more personal than political.

Such a psychological shift is expected, for the reader is witnessing once again the great magnetic power of the myth of the Southern gentleman. When father and son dispute over the son's romance, they use the same political terms of reference. Page is far more secure in this kind of conflict than he would be in a political conflict because, as the reader senses throughout the novel, nothing is really at stake:

"Not so, sir," retorted the Major. "It is true, and I do speak of my own knowledge: even the negroes are talking about it [Bruce Landon's romance with Margaret Reid]. It is a disgrace; and whether you go to Europe or not, I forbid you ever to go again to that place. You cannot be going to marry the young woman, and I will not stand any disgrace. If I hear of you doing

anything disgraceful I will cut you off with a shilling. What is
more, I will not have my name dragged into the mire of low
scandal-mongering, and if you go again, you go at your peril."
He turned to leave.

Bruce's face turned white.

"You do not know what you are talking about. I am a
gentleman."

The Major made a gesture.

"I refuse to be dictated to as if I were a negro," said the young
man. "I will go wherever and whenever I please."

"At your peril." (III, 198-99)

The Major's objection to this poor girl is of course severely
modified once he meets her; for he discovers that she is a lady.
But he does not give his approval to the marriage until he learns
that Mr. Browne is actually his brother and that the girl "has a
name and blood as good as" his own. "She is Charles Landon's
great-grand-daughter" (III, 257). This is one of those preposterous conclusions that one finds in nineteenth-century sentimental fiction. Page, unable to reconcile the differences in the
social caste of his lovers, draws upon the stock device of revealing the mysterious and unknown ancestry of his poor heroine.
There is no other way of rendering her status than by giving her
social prestige, a pedigree, and a heritage of note; for, once he
describes Margaret as a lady, he has to invent for her a past that
will be responsible for her noble character.

On Newfound River has most of the faults of Page's fiction,
but the sentimentality, plot contrivances, the stock characters,
and rhetorical bombast do not control the narrative nor diminish
its power. The novel, in fact, is one of the author's more substantial productions; and it is written with a stylistic grace that
seems effortless and from a point of view that remains objective
and consistent throughout most of the book. The minor characters, who in his fiction are usually Dickensian characters with a
Southern accent, function thematically; they form a kind of
chorus to the main action of the book. Pokeberry, "who had
come to the neighborhood a few years before" and whose "only
ostensible occupation was hunting" runaway Negroes is plausible
and amusing when kept a local-color character rather than a
sinister antagonist—he remains the opportunistic type until the
end of the novel when Page manipulates him into the unlikely
role of villain. Sam Mills, a friend of Major Landon's; Hall, the

Constable; Squire Johnson, the judge, who admits he would have decided a legal case against Major Landon because the latter is a Whig; Dick Runaway, the lazy but faithful Negro who ultimately captures his pursuer, Pokeberry—all of these caricatures give vitality and versimilitude to a traditionally sentimental novel; moreover, they root the action to its locale and its time.

IV "Elsket"

The South was not the only subject of Page's fiction. Periodically he turned to other locales and attempted folk tales that emulated the oral epics of ancient times. His most successful achievement in this genre is "Elsket," a story he published in *Scribner's Magazine* in August, 1891. An agreeable fantasy, "Elsket" describes an exotic village in the Norwegian mountains where Olaf and his daughter Elsket, the last of her race, live. The girl has been waiting for a letter—the reader is not told from whom—but is disappointed as her father repeatedly returns without mail from a larger city in the valley. Page tells nothing of why Elsket suffers or why she feels such loneliness, and he gives the early sections of the story an air of mystery. This restraint seems proper, for the narrator is foreign to this Norwegian mountain village, and the people do not reveal their secrets quickly. Soon, however, the mysterious past of Elsket unfolds, and the reader learns that she nursed to health and fell in love with a young man who had recently visited her village. The love affair was never consummated, for the Englishman—a Saxon whose "blood" is aristocratic—was murdered by his rival, a lifelong friend and lover of Elsket. Elsket awaits the return of her Englishman from his native land, where he went to disentangle himself from a love affair at home; she is unaware of his death and she herself wastes away and dies. She is buried by her father in her bridal gown.

The aspect of Elsket's character that Page wants the reader to admire is her quiet demonstration of loyalty and fidelity, qualities which distinguish all of his heroes and heroines. As with so many of his exotic romantic tales that are not concerned with the South, Page spoils his effect by hurrying through too many incidents; he tells them to the reader rather than dramatically rendering them. All the people are seen at second hand, and there is no highlighting of scene or character. Nevertheless, the story has certain commendable qualities. It is told in a biblical style suited to the supernatural mood of the subject; and this unreal village, buried in the snow of the Norwegian hills, is exotically evoked, a fit setting for the fantasy that takes place. The sense of doom that pervades Olaf and his daughter, and the heavy loneliness and loyalty of the latter, are the best features of the story—one truly believes, within the context of the created fantasy, that Elsket is the last of her race and that with her death this once prosperous village will no longer exist. The mood and attitude that Page brought to those early stories in which the Southern hero died and with him the end of a great civilization is used to telling effect in "Elsket"; and, although the reader does not feel the historical truth present in the Southern stories, he is moved by the identification of the heroine with her race, with her land. And the grievance of the father for his daughter is described with a tragic dignity necessary for such a tale.

V *The Southern Human Comedy*

"Elsket" is set in a Norwegian mountain village, but its themes of unrealized love and loyalty and its emphasis on those racial characteristics that are "bred in the bone" mark it as a tale very similar to Page's more traditional fiction. In the same year that he published "Elsket" (1891) and throughout the early 1890's, he returned repeatedly to these considerations in a series of stories whose theme is the significance of pedigree. He makes the constant distinction between lineage, which inevitably reveals the manner of the man, and wealth, which is an incidental acquirement. The opening paragraphs of "Run to Seed," a story published in the same issue of *Scribner's Magazine* as "Elsket," tells of the moral and social legacy inherited by one Southern boy, the legacy that will help him to overcome his poverty:

> Jim's father died at Gettysburg; up against the Stone Fence; went to heaven in a chariot of fire on that fateful day when the issue between the two parts of the country was decided: when the slaughter on the Confederate side was such that after the battle a lieutenant was in charge of a regiment, and a major commanded a brigade.
> This fact was much to Jim, though no one knew it: it tempered his mind: ruled his life. He never remembered the time when he did not know the story of his mother, in her worn black

dress and with her pale face, used to tell him of the bullet-dented sword and faded red sash which hung on the chamber wall. (II, 137)

The hero is the son of "the poorest people in the neighborhood. Everybody was poor; for the county lay in the track of the armies, and the war had swept the country as clean as a floor. But the Uptons were the poorest even in that community" (II, 137). Realizing that his family has "run to seed," Jim takes a job on the railway and ultimately dies in an accident—but only after he has rescued a young girl and proven his courage. The point of the story is that Jim's family has indeed gone to seed but, as one character announces, " 'Gentleman, it was d—d good seed!' " The paramount qualities of honor and courage have lingered in spite of his family's poverty.

Other tales, written during this same period, are less direct yet no less insistent on the significance of lineage. "My Cousin Fanny" (December, 1892) is more a character sketch than a story, more an evocation of the past than a tale of conflict that is set in the past. "We do not keep Christmas now as we used to do in Old Hanover," Page begins; and once again he brings us into that familiar, sentimentalized past, that golden age before the Civil War. He writes an unpretentious, low-keyed tale, a reminiscence of his Cousin Fanny who was an eccentric, hypochondriacal old woman whom the family gently teased. This is the kind of sketch that he is particularly fond of writing, for it combines those ingredients—bucolic peace and odd, senti-mentalized characters—that are associated only with joy in his mind; there is no real threat to the quiet life presented and so the tale is written without the anguish that one feels in *Red Rock* or *Gordon Keith* or the more political stories.

Beyond the tender character sketch that he creates, there is little else in "My Cousin Fanny" except the glimpses into the author's youth—his early reading of Scott; his happy childhood in Hanover, Virginia; his warm and affectionate relationship with his early, influential teacher, Cousin Fanny. As one reads this early fiction—even so slight a sketch as "My Cousin, Fanny" —one feels his desire to develop out of his native surroundings a kind of vast human comedy, a panoramic view of life before the Civil War in Virginia; but Page does not have the imaginative vision of Balzac or Faulkner. And he really does not care about

his people beyond their manners and their customs, beyond the
roles they play as types in a vanished drama.

One stock type is the Civil War veteran who, in the Reconstruction period, finds himself lost and without purpose. The
hero of "The Gray Jacket of No. 4" (1892) is a drunkard who
has sacrificed his farm and all his worldly possessions—all except
the gray jacket that represents the connection with his own past
glory in the war. His attachment to the jacket is obsessive and
almost mad—indeed, his obsession is plausible fundamentally because he is a drunkard and partially mad. Once brave, once
aware of why he fought, he holds onto his jacket as if it retains
the one remnant of reality he still knows. But he is thoroughly
disoriented and bewildered in a defeated South; ultimately, he
drives himself completely insane.

The aspect of madness in the story is credible and even
poignant. But Page confuses his point of view by taking on the
passions of his mad hero. Thus when Lee's monument is un-
veiled in Richmond and No. 4 is selected during the parade to
carry the colors as a tribute to his heroism in the war, Page
interrupts the narrative to eulogize the South; and whatever
distance has been maintained between No. 4 and the narrator is
blurred by the blind chauvinism of the author:

> But this was merely the outward image [the pageantry of the
> parade]; the real fact was the spirit. It was the South. It was
> the spirit of the South; not of the new South, not yet merely of
> the old South, but the spirit of the great South. When the young
> troops from every Southern State marched by in their fresh
> uniforms, with well-drilled batallions, there were huzzas, much
> applause, and enthusiasm; when the old soldiers came there was
> a tempest: wild cheers choking with sobs and tears, the well-
> known, once-heard-never-forgotten cry of the battling South,
> known in history as "the rebel yell." Men and women and
> children joined in it. It began at the first sight of the regular
> column, swelled up the crowded streets, rose to the thronged
> housetops, ran along them for squares like a conflagration, and
> then came rolling back in volume only to rise and swell again
> greater than before. Men wept; children shrilled; women sobbed
> aloud. What was it! Only a thousand or two of old or aging men
> riding or tramping along through the dust of the street, under
> some old flags, dirty and ragged and stained. But they rep-
> resented the spirit of the South; they represented the spirit which
> when honor was in question never counted the cost; the spirit

that had stood up for the South against overwhelming odds for four years, and until the South had crumbled and perished under the forces of war; the spirit that is the strongest guaranty to us to-day that the Union is and is to be; the spirit that, glorious in victory, had displayed a fortitude yet greater in defeat. (II, 235-36)

The parade revives in No. 4 a certain sobriety, and for a while he works well; but soon he is thoroughly mad, and claims in his last delirious moments that he has betrayed his honor by selling his gray jacket. He does sell the jacket, and the narrator makes certain that he is given a soldier's burial; he buys the jacket from a shopman and buries No. 4 in his Civil War uniform.

The story is not clearly focused, but the idea—that of Southern honor unable to sustain itself in the midst of defeat—is suggestive. Moreover, this theme recurs in many of the tales and most elaborately in *Red Rock* and *Gordon Keith*. The breakdown of the South that Page knew as a boy, the end of a special kind of heroism in the post-bellum South, was a traumatic defeat and loss that he could never fully absorb; and, as a consequence, the conclusions of many stories are extreme and contrived, as if the author cannot control them: madness in "The Gray Jacket of No. 4," political conversion in *Red Rock*, death in dozens of stories— death before the hero has to live in the defeated South and suffer the humiliation of Northern and Negro dominance.

Other stories extend the dimensions of the human comedy. In "P'Laski's Tunament" (1890), Page presents an eccentric old Negro father who has had many wives and children and who treats his present wife and child contemptuously. In "Miss Dangerlie's Roses" (1892), the Southern hero reappears, dedicated to be like his father "if he was not," and remembering "all that his mother had told him of his gentleness, his high courtesy, his faithfulness, his devotion to duty, his unselfishness" (II, 343). Even when the heroine, Miss Dangerlie, and her lover deceive him, he exhibits the most generous and noble behavior. In "How the Captain Made Christmas" (1893), the heroic veteran of the war helps a young Southerner win his lady.

During this same period Page published innumerable sketches and anecdotes, originally written to meet the exacting requirements of *Harper's* "Editor's Drawer," which he collected in 1894 and published as *Pastime Stories*. In the preface to the volume in the Plantation Edition, Page admits "that no one will be as sensible of the demerits of these stories as I am myself"; these sketches "have survived for generations . . . and if they do not read well, it is because I have marred them in the telling." His one hope is to excite the reader's "curiosity so far as to make [him] go back to that early and delightful chronicle of old Virginia life" (X, xi-xii).

The anecdotes do not read well, although one must add that they have effects that would be better appreciated through an oral delivery. Their subjects are deliberately lighthearted and trivial. In one group—generally about the Negro—Page presents those endearing characteristics of the loyal slave: "Ole Sue" (1892) traces the affection of a Negro for his mule; "Israel's Bargain" (1892) considers a lovable Negro who steals from college students; "A Story of Charley Harris" (1893) presents the faithful body-servant of Colonel Carter of Cartersville, who was so realistic an actor that everyone mistook him for an actual thief; "How Andrews Carried the Precinct" (1893) considers a loyal servant's help in defeating his white master's political opponent, a post-war, militant Negro. Other sketches in this group pursue similar themes: "Rasmus" (1893) repeats the subject of "Old Sue," a Negro's attachment to his mule; in "Her Great-Grandmother's Ghost" (1893), a girl of twenty-two returns to her family home, where her grandmother had died at the age of twenty-two, only to find the ancestor's Negro butler—in this Hawthornesque story, the girl identifies with the grandmother and asks to die like her forebear; "Rachel's Loves" treats of one Negro outduping the other, a superstitious drunkard, for the hand of Rachel (here the Negroes are simple and foolish, and the author's condescending attitude toward them is offensive); "How Jinny Eased Her Mind" (1893) again presents Negroes as lovable and irresponsible—Jinny is imprisoned for hitting her husband, but the jury reverses the decision when he asks to be sent away with her.

A second group of sketches deals with the author's experiences as a lawyer. In "He Would Have Gotten a Lawyer" (1893), a Negro is ungrateful for his lawyer's defense of his felony and escapes from the jail at night; in "When Little Mordecai Was at the Bar" (1892), Page evokes nostalgia by considering Little Mordecai's legal feats; in "The Prosecution of Mrs. Dullet" (1893), a judge dissuades Mr. Dullet from putting his wife into a penitentiary because she has forged his signature, permitting their daughter to marry someone of whom he disapproves; in "He Knew What Was Due to the Court" (1893), a dissipated, insane man tries to hold on to his property.

These pastime stories are clearly trivial; and, as Page suggests in his preface, if they have any merit it must be evident itself in the oral transmission. One point is important to make and that is the author's depiction of a surprising number of obtuse and superstitious, drunken and thieving Negroes. As Harriet Holman has remarked, "according to erroneous popular opinion, Page's stories are full of faithful, discreet, self-effacing Negro servants like Sam, old Billy, Unc Edinburg, and Mammy Krenda, but for sheer number the Jim Crow type of character ridiculing the Negro overshadows them."[20] In *Pastime Stories* this type of Negro recurs, and he functions as a kind of clown in Page's human comedy.

The *Pastime Stories* are more sketches than stories, more depictions of caricature than character, more whimsical anecdotes than elaborate descriptions of a fallen civilization. Of greater importance than any of these tales are three stories that Page wrote in 1894—stories that return thematically to his earlier work. "The Burial of the Guns," "Little Darby," and "The Old Gentleman of the Black Stock" also come to terms with the effect that the Civil War has had on the South.

VI *The Vanished Glory*

"The Burial of the Guns," although a weak story, reveals most clearly Page's over-all attitude toward the South and the Civil War. The guns that are buried (by a company of Confederate soldiers) are of course Southern guns, and the burial is that of the South's hopes for ever winning the war. As Page describes these weapons, they seem almost human and animistic; they certainly are more human than the characters themselves. This observation is not surprising, for in "The Burial of the Guns" the author is not really interested in people or guns but in what they represent, in the concept that they dramatize. In this case, the guns symbolize the Southern honor and duty and loyalty—in a word, the Southern heroism—that have been overcome but not destroyed.

The loss of the guns is the loss of great dignity and power—almost, the reader is made to feel, a sexual power. It is a loss that is greater than that of human beings, more significant and transcending than that of human beings; and as Page extols this superhuman quality, he himself grows curiously inhuman: "Most of the men who were not killed were retaken before the day was over, with many guns; but the Cat was lost. She remained in enemy's hands and probably was being turned against her old comrades and lovers. The company was inconsolable. The death of comrades was too natural and common a thing to depress the men beyond what such occurrences necessarily did; but to lose a gun! It was like losing the old Colonel: it was worse: a gun was ranked as a brigadier: and the Cat was equal to a major-general. The other guns seemed lost without her . . ." (II, 13).

What counts is not so much the human beings who have been lost on the battlefield but the honor with which these human beings have fought and died. Page tells us of the effects of the Civil War—and they are certainly harrowing—but he never demonstrates dramatically the suffering of individual people; the result is experience rendered at second hand:

> The minds of the men seemed to go back to the time when they were not so alone, but were part of a great and busy army, and some of them fell to talking of the past, and the battles they had figured in, and of the comrades they had lost. They told them off in a slow and colorless way, as if it were all part of the great past as much as the dead they named. One hundred and nineteen times they had been in action. Only seventeen men were left of the eighty odd who had first enlisted in the battery, and of these four were at home crippled for life. Two of the oldest men had been among the half-dozen who had fallen in the skirmish just the day before. It looked tolerably hard to be killed that way after passing for four years through such battles as they had been in; and both had wives and children at home, too, and not a cent to leave them to their names. They agreed calmly that they'd have to "sort of look after them a little" if they ever got home. These were some of the things they talked about as they pulled their old worn coats about them, stuffed their thin, weather-stained hands in their ragged pockets to warm them, and squatted down under the breastwork to keep a little out of the wind. (II, 26-27)

What the reader witnesses in "The Burial of the Guns" is pathos evoked at the moment of death; and he is reminded, once

again, of the great propensity that Page has for death in his
fiction, the frequency with which he presents his Southern hero
dying in the moment of a glory that is certain to vanish. In this
tale, the guns are the hero; and before they are dropped into the
water, before the troops disband, the Colonel utters what is
really a prayer and a eulogy:

> My men, I cannot let you go so. We were neighbors when the
> war began—many of us, and some not here to-night; we have
> been more since then—comrades in arms; we have all stood for
> one thing—for Virginia and the South; we have all done our duty
> —tried to do our duty; we have fought a good fight, and now it
> seems to be over, and we have been overwhelmed by number, not
> whipped—and we are going home. We have the future before us
> —we don't know just what it will bring, but we can stand a good
> deal. We have proved it. Upon us depends the South in the
> future as in the past. You have done your duty in the past, you
> will not fail in the future. Go home and be honest, brave, self-
> sacrificing, God-fearing citizens, as you have been soldiers, and
> you need not fear for Virginia and the South. The war may be
> over; but you will ever be ready to serve your country. The end
> may not be as we wanted it, prayed for it, fought for it; but we
> can trust God; the end in the end will be the best that could
> be; even if the South is not free she will be better and stronger
> that she fought as she did. Go home and bring up your children
> to love her, and though you may have nothing else to leave
> them, you can leave them the heritage that they are sons of men
> who were in Lee's army. (II, 35-36)

This speech, idealistic and biased, chauvinistic and parochial,
can be duplicated by similar quotations from the most sophisticated Southern authors of the post-Civil War period. It indicates, for one thing, that Page was not always successful in
keeping the detachment of which he perennially boasts in so many
stories and essays, and it contradicts the assertion often made
that local color-fiction was disinterested and unconcerned with
political issues. The Colonel's speech depends for its effects on
the assumption that words like *duty, honest, brave, self-
sacrificing,* and *God-fearing* are meaningful to these unsuccessful soldiers after all that they have been through; it also implies
that the abstractions are intrinsically more important than the
soldiers whom the Colonel addresses. Although Page is unaware
of his final effect, this dedication to abstractions has led, in a

curious way, to the abdication of human relations, and the connection between the individual and Virginia or the South or honor has assumed transcendent significance.

The whites honor these abstractions in other whites and more importantly in the Negro. The faithful colored man knows this axiom of Southern heroism intuitively and so never insists on his freedom, never insists on being considered a human being. In a story like "Burial of the Guns," the quality of idealism is strained to an extreme point so that it is difficult to conceive of the war as having been fought by individual people. At the end of the tale, which has concerned itself fundamentally with those moments after Appomattox when the guns must be buried, the soldiers include in the burial rites the names of the guns that they have used in combat. Those names—Matthew, Mark, Luke, John, The Eagle, and The Cat—are pointedly Christian. The implication is clear: the war these soldiers have fought has been not only religious in nature but also in the service of the highest possible cause in their lives—the honor of the South.

"Little Darby," a story in the same vein, retells the well-known anecdote that served as the source of "Marse Chan." But in "Little Darby" Page is closer to the original material than in the more compressed and suggestive early version: the girl's letter that warns the hero, "Don't come home without a furlough," takes on greater significance, and the individual families do not have the aristocratic bearing of those in "Marse Chan"— they are poor-whites. The serenity of Virginia, the threat of oncoming war, and the rival families recall those similar elements in "Marse Chan" and the other stories of *In Ole Virginia;* in "Little Darby," however, Page intends to testify to the sectional loyalty of the lower classes during the Civil War. He attempts to demonstrate that heroism can exist among the poor as well as the rich, but in the process of writing the story he cannot avoid making class distinctions—Darby descends from a tradition of noble Englishmen, and his pedigree accounts for his courage during the war. Arthur Hobson Quinn, in a sympathetic estimation of Page's fiction, makes a similar point and reprints a long, significant letter that "explains the genesis of 'Little Darby' and also of his earliest stories":

I have no doubt that your estimate of the comparative merits of my short stories and of my novels is absolutely correct and I have a secret fear that my earlier stories, those in dialect, are superior in their appeal to any that I have written since. If I find you selecting "Marse Chan" and "Meh Lady" in preference to "Edinburg's Drowndin'" and "Polly," I have no right to complain and it brings me to a reflection which I have always had: as to what is the secret of the success of the story or novel. Is it the theme or the art with which any theme, reasonably broad, is handled, or is it something growing out of the union of the two? Personally I have always estimated "Edinburg's Drowndin'" as possibly the broadest of my stories, at least as the one giving a reflection of the broadest current of the old Southern life, and so far as literary art is concerned, it seems to me at least on a par with the others. I think, therefore, it must be the unrelieved tragedy in "Marse Chan" or the fact that "Meh Lady" appealed to both sides, and was written to make this appeal, that has given them a prestige, if I may use so important a word, far beyond that of "Edinburg's Drowndin'" and "Ole 'Stracted." "Little Darby," "Run to Seed" and "Elsket," which you have signalized with the stamp of your imprimatur, I also think among the very best stories I have written. The first two of these appeal to me almost as much as the dialect stories. The first of these was written on precisely the same theme with "Marse Chan" and out of the consciousness that whereas the tragedy of "Marse Chan" was laid in the highest social rank, the incident which had given rise to it was based on a letter written by a poor girl, of much lower rank, to her lover, who like "Marse Chan" had found his death on the battle-field, and I felt somehow that it was due to that class that I should testify with whatever power I might possess, to their devotion to the South. If there is a difference it seems to me that it lies rather in the fact that readers estimate as more romantic a tragedy in the upper ranks of life than in lower, whereas, we know that rank has nothing to do with it.[21]

In the early part of "Little Darby," the pre-war South—and, more specifically, pre-war Virginia—is presented as a quiet, rural area. Political differences are the only cause for excitement, and the opposing political positions are made clear: they represent secession and national unity. Little Darby, whose family favors secession, is separated from Vashti, the girl he loves, because of the political differences of their families. When he enlists in the army, she does not permit herself to yield to him although she confesses her love to her mother. Page gives the situation the chivalric overtones that are present in his other fiction: like lovers in a courtly romance, the warrior leaves to defend his lady despite the fact that the lady rejects him.

But Darby is not so heroic in battle as those protagonists of the earlier stories in spite of Page's desire "to testify" to his "devotion to the South." He is described as a poor-white without breeding; and though the author brings compassion to his tale, he does not assume the same attitude of admiration that he maintains toward those Southern heroes who have a more aristocratic pedigree. Consequently, Little Darby is more credible and realistic though he is smaller in scope than the figures of *In Ole Virginia*. He is inconspicuous as a soldier—taciturn, loyal, brave, but largely unnoticed—and Page puts him into a company of common soldiers whom he describes with restraint: "The war was very different from what those who went into it expected it to be. Until it had gone on some time it seemed mainly marching and camping and staying in camp, quite uselessly as seemed to many, and drilling and doing nothing. Much of the time— especially later on—was given to marching and getting food; but drilling and camp duties at first took up most of it. This was especially hard on the poorer men, no one knew what it was to them. Some moped, some fell sick" (II, 84-85).

Equally successful is the description of the women who stayed at home and suffered appalling poverty. Once again the mood described is credible because it is not excessive:

> . . . the women of the district had a hungry time, and the war bore on them heavily as on everyone else, and as it went on they suffered more and more. Many a woman went day after day and week after week without even the small portion of coarse cornbread which was ordinarily her common fare. They called oftener and oftener at the houses of their neighbors who owned the plantations near them, and always received something; but as time went on the plantations themselves were stripped; the little things they could take with them when they went, such as eggs, honey, etc., were wanting, and to go too often without anything to give might make them seem like beggars, and that they were not. Their husbands were in the army fighting for the South, as well as those from the plantations, and they stood by this fact on the same level.
>
> The arrogant looks of the negroes were unpleasant, and in marked contrast to the universal graciousness of their owners, but they were slaves and they could afford to despise them. Only they must uphold their independence. Thus no one outside knew

what the women of the district went through. When they wrote
to their husbands or sons that they were in straits, it meant that
they were starving. Such a letter meant all the more because
they were used to hunger, but not to writing, and a letter meant
perhaps days of thought and enterprise and hours of labor.
(II, 93-94)

Against this bleak background, the simple action of the story
rises. It turns upon the hero's demonstration of honor to his lady,
a demonstration that is all the more impressive for the circumstances that surround it. The lady, Vashti, finally confesses her
love to Darby and writes that his mother is ill, that "he ought to
get a furlough and come home, and when he did she would
marry him." The letter, however, contains one crucial proviso:

> At the end of the letter, as if possibly she thought, in the great-
> ness of her relief at her confession, that the temptation she held
> out might prove too great even for him, or possibly only because
> she was a woman, there was a postscript scrawled across the
> coarse, blue Confederate paper: "Don't come without a furlough;
> for if you don't come honorable I won't marry you." This, how-
> ever, Darby scarcely read. His being was in the letter. It was
> only later that the picture of his mother ill and failing came to
> him, and it smote him in the midst of his happiness and clung
> to him afterward like a nightmare. It haunted him. She was
> dying. (II, 102-3)

Darby does not wait for his furlough; when he meets Vashti,
her first word is "Darby," uttered in surprise and love for the
returned hero. When the subsequent conversation reveals that
he has returned to his dying mother without a leave, Vashti
accuses him of being a coward and a deserter, of having forsaken
his honor. Honor at this point is more important than Darby
himself, who grows sick and delirious because of the rejection.
Ultimately, he redeems himself by dying for the South and for
his heartless Lady, thus accepting the grounds on which
Vashti has denied him: he prevents Northern soldiers from shoot-
ing Vashti, who is in the process of burning a bridge to prevent
the Northern company from concluding a raid. Darby drowns, a
fitting martyr to the abstract glory that Vashti has demanded
of him.

"Little Darby" is still another retelling of that stock sentimental situation in which the hero dies in battle for his lady; and its power relies upon the dedication of the two central figures to abstractions that transcend their own humanity. Neither Little Darby nor Vashti doubts for a moment that honor transcends their individual importance; and the popularity of this tale—as well as many others like it—assumes the reader's implication in the myth of heroism, the belief in such abstractions as honor and courage.

A third story, "The Old Gentleman of the Black Stock" (1894), is not concerned with the war; it develops, in a quiet and attractive manner, some of the author's favorite themes: the superiority of the country to the city, of the past to the present, of feeling to intellect. This tale, one of Page's most popular ones, is an autobiographical recounting of his first experiences in Richmond twenty years earlier. The young lawyer's uncertainty and lack of sophistication are well presented, and his sentimental love affair, though traditional and predictable, is restrained. Most effective, however, is the description of "the old gentleman of the black stock" through whom the central ideas become evident. His life has been an economic success but an emotional failure largely because of one great fault—selfishness. "I made one mistake, sir," he tells the narrator, "early in life, and it has lasted me ever since. I put Brains before everything, Intellect before Heart. It was all selfishness: that was the rock on which I split. I was a man of parts, sir, and I thought with my intellect I could do everything. But I could not" (VIII, 112-13).

The old man serves as the narrator's literary and moral mentor. Having sacrificed love for the acquisition of money and the "selflessness" of family life for his own personal goals, he has since depended on books for comfort. Through the "old gentleman of the black stock," Page expresses some of his own observations on literature:

> I asked him about Carlyle and Emerson, for I was just then discovering them. He admitted the sincerity of both; but Carlyle he did not like.
> "He is always ill-tempered and sour, and is forever sneering at others. He is Jeremiah, without his inspiration or his occasion," he said of him. "He is not a gentleman, sir, and has never forgiven either the world or himself for it."

"Do you think he writes well?" I demanded.

"Yes, sir, he writes vigorously,—I suppose you mean that,—but it is not English. I do not know just what to term it. It was a trick with him, a part of his pedantry. But when I want acerbity I prefer Swift."

Emerson he put on a much higher place than Carlyle; but though he admitted his sincerity, and ranked him as the first American literary man, he did not read him much.

"He is a kindly man," he said, "and has 'wrought in a sad sincerity.' But he preaches too much for me, and he is all texts. When I want preaching I go to church." (VIII, 41-42)

Books can never supplant the emotional loss that the old gentleman has suffered—"they forsake you," he complains as he dies, "or bore you" (VIII, 108)—and he warns the young lawyer to "cultivate the affections. Take an old man's word for it, that the men who are happy are those who love and are loved. Better love the meanest thing that lives than only yourself" (VIII, 116). The narrator takes the man's advice and marries the daughter of the woman whom the "old gentleman" had given up years before.

This sentimental tale was so popular in its time because it satisfies all the demands of the popular romance: it presents love lost in the "old gentleman of the black stock" and love redeemed in the young lawyer; it emphasizes the triumph of the heart over the head, for the young lawyer wins his young lady through self-sacrifice and devotion; and it offers a tribute to the purity and innocence of rural life, for both the hero and heroine have just come from the country.

"The Burial of the Guns," "Little Darby," and "The Old Gentleman of the Black Stock" appeared in 1894. Page did not publish another work of fiction until 1898 when *Red Rock*, his most important novel, appeared serially in *Scribner's Magazine*. The human comedy that he had traced in "Run to Seed" and *On Newfound River* surrendered to the more tragic, more poignant, vanished glory of "The Burial of the Guns" and "Little Darby." None of these stories was so impressive as those he first published, and they all suggest a deliquescence of the clear point of view and tone in "Marse Chan" and "Meh Lady."

In the period from 1894 to 1898 Page struggled with *Red Rock;* in this elaborate, ambitious novel—the finest one that he wrote— he seeks to offer his ultimate defense of the South before and after the Civil War. As a work of art *Red Rock* does not succeed, for in spite of his attempt to be dispassionate and fair to both the North and the South, the book grows inevitably tendentious. As a defense of the South during Reconstruction, however, it remains one of the most impressive fictional accounts of the period.

CHAPTER 3

Reconstruction

*I*N OLE VIRGINIA was written out of love; the stories there-
after were an attempt to dramatize the human comedy of
the South. *Red Rock,* a duty and an act of loyalty, bears the
mark of careful writing, of objective, painful consideration that
is both its greatest merit and its worst defect. In the stories Page
could dream an ante-bellum South of his own creation, but in
Red Rock he felt obligated to record history as faithfully as
possible; as a consequence, the dream vanishes and becomes the
nightmare of Reconstruction. In *Red Rock,* he wrote his version
of the rape of the post-bellum South, and he wanted the novel
to stand in objective opposition to all those Northern accounts
(by Harriet Beecher Stowe, especially, but also by Albion W.
Tourgée and journalists like John T. Trowbridge and Sidney
Andrews) which pictured the South in unattractive terms. He
wanted his book to be the fullest and fairest description of Reconstruction—a "composite picture" of the time—but the defensive attitude he assumed mars the book. He could not achieve
the objectivity he sought, and in a letter that he wrote to Arthur
Hobson Quinn, he admitted his failure:

> It may interest you to know that when I first undertook to write
> "Red Rock," after having written a third or more of the novel
> I discovered that I had drifted into the production of a political
> tract. I bodily discarded what I had written, and going back
> beyond the War, in order to secure a background and a point of
> departure which would enable me to take a more serene path, I
> rewrote it entirely. I had discovered that the real facts in the
> Reconstruction period were so terrible that I was unable to
> describe them fully. The story of this period of National madness
> will doubtless be written some time and if any man will steep
> himself as I did, myself, in such records as the "Ku Klux Reports"

issued by the Government in 1872, and, "A Voice from South Carolina," published in Charleston in 1879; "The Prostrate State," and the newspapers of the reconstruction period I think he will agree with me in feeling that we are too near the time to be able to present the facts with true art.[1]

Red Rock, as Page realized, is not a successful novel; but in the literature of Reconstruction—so full of distorted, bitter accounts—it represents one of the few attempts at an objective rendering of the period. Although the book is inevitably biased, criticism of it is tempered by considering the almost impossible task he undertook. The author was too closely identified with all that had been lost and destroyed in the South to write the "comprehensive" novel of Reconstruction; but he did write the finest Southern version of this tragic era.

I   *The Ante-bellum South*

Page is wise to give the reader a view of ante-bellum times, for the placid pre-war life described in the first portion of the novel makes more real and pathetic the later grim pictures of Reconstruction. The title of the novel is significant, for it suggests the history of the plantation that is the setting of the novel and, by implication, of the South. The enormous rock that distinguishes this plantation from all others is red because of the blood shed on it by the first white woman of the area. This woman was the wife of Jacquelin Gray, the earliest American ancestor of the present Jacquelin Gray, who dominates the novel and represents the last scion of Southern nobility. The colonial woman was murdered by an Indian, and Page clearly indicates that her purity is archetypical; it serves as the model for later generations. Her current descendant, Miss Thomasia, a sister of Mr. Gray, is the great Southern lady, a goddess almost, who perpetuates the finest traditions of the South:

Even you, Miss or Madam [of the modern world], for all your silks and satins, cannot do it like Miss Thomasia. You are imitating the duchess you saw once, perhaps, in Hyde Park. The duchess would have imitated Miss Thomasia. You are at best an imitation; Miss Thomasia is the reality. Do not laugh at her, or call her provincial. She belongs to the realm where sincerity dwells and the heart still rules--the realm of old-time courtesy and high breeding, and you are the real provincial. It is a wide realm, though; and some day, if Heaven be good to you, you may reach it. But it must be by the highway of Sincerity and Truth. No other road leads there.[2]

In *Red Rock* and in many of the short stories Page deals with the same history and traditions of the South that Faulkner explores in his fiction, but his attitude toward that tradition is totally opposite in a historically significant way. The nineteenth-century author sees no further than the surface manners and customs, no deeper than the obvious stereotypes. For Page, the traditions passed on by the Gray family are never corrupted, never stained by miscegenation or by cruelty toward the Negro. He even suggests, through the superstitions of local residents, that Red Rock might have been the place where the Garden of Eden was located: "there were evidences that the Garden of Eden was situated not far from that spot, and certainly within the limits of the State" (IV, 47).

In this pre-war paradise youth and old age are dominant. The wise old men, the patriarchs of the plantation, are Jacquelin Gray and his cousin, Dr. Cary; and the innocent youths are their children, Jacquelin Gray and Blair Cary, the lovers of the novel. One other significant Southern character—perhaps the most significant character in the novel—emerges in these early pages, a boy called Steve Allen, whose father, together with the father of Jacquelin Gray, had fought in the Mexican War: "Steve Allen had come to Red Rock before Jacquelin could remember—the year after Steve's father was killed in Mexico, leading his company up the heights of Cerro Gordo, and his mother died of fever far down South. Mr. Gray had brought the boy home on his mother's death; so Steve was part of Red Rock" (IV, 7).

By having the fathers of his two youths fight in the Mexican War, Page demonstrates the loyalty of Southerners to the Union. The Grays and the Carys and the Allens despise war, and they are bitterly opposed to secession, to any war between the States. "Do you know what War is?" Dr. Cary tells a group of fire-eaters:

War is the most terrible of all disasters, except Dishonor. I do not speak of the dangers. For every brave man must face danger as it comes, and should court glory; and death for one's Country is glorious. I speak merely of the change that War inevitably brings. War is the destruction of everything that exists. You may fail or you may win, but what exists passes, and something different takes it place. The plough-share becomes a spear, and the pruning-hook a sword; the poor may become richer, but the rich must become poorer. You are the wealthiest people in the world to-day—not in mere riches, but in wealth. You may become the poorest. No people who enter a war wealthy and content ever come out of war so. I do not say that this is an unanswerable reason for not going to war. For war may be right at any cost. But it is not to be entered on unadvisedly or lightly; but in the fear of God. It should not be undertaken from mere enthusiasm; but deliberately, with a full recognition of its cost, and resolution to support its possible and direct consequences. (IV, 18-19)

II *The Forces that Bind the South*

When the war arrives, Cary and other anti-secessionists join with the Southern forces and fight honorably. Page does not present the war, assuming the reader's knowledge of it; he realized no doubt that there would be mixed motives in any sensible account that he might render and that his would not be the same sympathetic response which Northerners might bring to an account of Reconstruction. Furthermore, since he had never been in battle, he could only present the Civil War of the newspapers and of legend. Wisely, he focuses his attention on the post-war period when, as he reiterates with painful awareness, "everything like civil government had disappeared" (IV, 129).

The first act of Dr. Cary is to offer his newly freed servants a salary, but his Mammy reproaches him by saying, "I'm feared you'll charge me *bode* . . . I didn' do it for no wages" (IV, 148-49). The loyalty between servant and master is firm, and no degree of emancipation will weaken that relationship. The Negro in Page's fiction does not want freedom; he thinks that his servile role is perfectly honorable, placing him in a Southern hierarchy of which he is proud. This relationship is central in the novel, and it contrasts ironically with the rebellious attempts of those misguided Negroes who are goaded on by Radical Republicans.

Loyalty is a significant and basic characteristic of the Southern hero, and it exists in all his relationships. The friendship between Steve Allen and Jacquelin Gray, for example, is one that is at least as great as that of love, and like love it develops from the author's chivalric code of Southern heroism.

As time went on, a shadow began to fall between Jacquelin and the sun. Steve was in love with Blair. Steve was always with her; his name was always on her lips, and hers frequently on his. She rode his horse; and he often came to Red Rock with her. And as Jacquelin watched, he knew he had no chance. It cut deeper than anyone ever knew; but Jacquelin fought it out and won. He would not let it come between him and Steve. Steve had always been like a brother. He would still love Blair. This was not forbidden him. Not every knight always won his great love. It was the loyalty, not the success, that was knightly. If she loved Steve, he could make her happier than Jacquelin himself ever could have done. And Jacquelin, if God gave him power, would rejoice with them in time. (IV, 235-36)

The friendship between Steve Allen and Jacquelin Gray is the strongest relationship in the novel, far stronger than any relationship either boy has with Blair Cary. Page emphasizes their attachment and mutual dependency, for later in the novel it permits both of them, grown to manhood, to defend the South against carpetbaggers and scalawags.

Another relationship that is significant is that of Miss Thomasia and Steve Allen. In love with his father years before, Miss Thomasia eventually rejected him because of "two besetting sins —drink and gambling"; as a consequence of her disappointment, she never married. In ante-bellum times she guides Steve so that he will forego the venial "sins" of his father. Miss Thomasia, as Steve recognizes, is unique—"there aren't any of 'em like you nowadays. They don't make 'em so any more. The mould's broken" (IV, 255). With her high moral criteria, her inflexible code of honorable behavior, she is the proper mentor for the Southern hero. Unsullied, pure, virginal, she represents for all the men in the novel, but especially for Steve Allen, the ideality of Southern womanhood. Page gives this relationship a religious, mystical tone that goes beyond words: it is one in which Miss Thomasia suggests the figure of Mary and Steve Allen that of Christ. Certainly Steve Allen is crucified by carpetbaggers and Radical Republicans; by the end of the novel, he is a genuine martyr to the South.

The love story presents the last important relationship among the Southerners in the novel—the inevitable triangle of the two lovers, Steve Allen and Jacquelin Gray, and their independent lady, Blair Cary. It is a sexless affair, as usual in Page's fiction, and recurs intermittently as a counterpoint to the more sober, historical sections of the book. The young lady, who models herself after Miss Thomasia, has those standard characteristics of the Southern lady: an inexorable pride that is incomprehensible to Northerners; a compassion for the Negroes; an absolute loyalty to the Southern gentleman; and ineffable beauty. Eventually she marries Jacquelin Gray, but only after he has developed into a model Southern gentleman worthy of her high standards. Through the two lovers, Red Rock, which serves as a microcosm of the South itself, is perpetuated for later generations.

The various relationships of these Southerners—the close ties between father and son, the friendship of two boys, the powerful love a Southern lady feels for her surrogate son, the romance of the Southern gentleman and his lady, the mutual love that all white Southerners have for one another—intertwine like strands of a rope to form an indomitable civilization that will not tolerate Northerners who have come to the South for personal aggrandizement. Against the high rectitude of the Southerners are measured the various motives of emigrant Northerners, and the clash that inevitably ensues forms the tension of the novel.

Page's Northerners are generally of two types: those who have adopted the role of conqueror and intend to rape the South, and those who show great sympathy for the South and voluntarily become a part of Southern life. There is no attempt at depicting character, and the contrasts are sharp and often ludicrous. Figures like Hiram Still, a scalawag, and Jonadab Leech, a carpetbagger, are so patently evil they never emerge as more than representatives of a distinct type. Still is a poor white who has a bond for Red Rock and intends to take it over; one of the central strands in the novel concerns the legal war between Still and Jacquelin Gray, in which Still's bond ultimately proves to be fraudulent. It is impossible to believe in this conflict, for Still is so corrupt that he has no redeeming virtues: he refuses, for example, to bury Jacquelin Gray's mother beside his father and only after great and repeated threats does he acquiesce. "If many overseers succeeded in routing their masters by similar transparent infamies," a contemporary reviewer justly argued, "that is the saddest testimony to the exhaustion of the old South in both courage and capacity."[3] Still, in trying to acquire Red Rock, is attempting to pillage the South of all its material and moral values. Moreover, it is symptomatic of the author's attitude that Still's closest friend should be a carpetbagger.

This other villain, Jonadab Leech, whose name suggests the vulgar extremity of Page's conception, arrives "one afternoon with only a carpetbag" and takes charge of the freedmen. Leech is a typical carpetbagger of Southern fiction; other examples of the stereotype are found in Joel Chandler Harris's *Gabriel Tolliver*, in Thomas Dixon's *The Leopard's Spots* and *The Clansman*, and in most of the Southern literature of Reconstruction. Page makes Leech "one of the leading men of the State," a greedy opportunist who boasts "that he owned his own country. Carried it in his breeches pocket, he said" (IV, 372). The portrayal of the carpetbagger is a caricature. Page undercuts his intentions by projecting an antagonist whom the reader can finally think of as only amusing. Whatever one's interpretation of Reconstruction may be, it is clear that Radical Republicans were not driven by the simple, crass motives Pages gives to Jonadab Leech. The author's view of Reconstruction is a very simple one and herein lies the chief fault of the novel: the characters—especially the antagonists—are not people at all but sentimental types. When Page writes of Leech, he is incapable of being objective or even tolerant, and the novel loses its tension, the very real and complex conflict that historically had occurred between the Radical Republicans and the white Southerners:

> The amount of spoil which in time was found to be divided was something of which not even Leech himself, at first, had any idea. The railways, the public printing, insurance, and all internal improvements, were fertile fields for the exercise of his genius. He was shortly an undisputed power. He followed his simple rule: he led. When someone offered a resolution to put down new matting in the Assembly hall, Leech amended to substitute Brussels carpet. To prove his liberality he added mahogany furniture, and handsome pier-glasses. The bills went up into the scores of thousands; but that was nothing. . . . If rumors were true, not only did Leech not pay the bills, he partly received their proceeds. His aspirations were growing every day. He had no trouble in carrying his measures through. He turned his committee-room—or one of his rooms, for he had several—into a saloon, where he kept whiskey, champagne, and cigars always

free for those who were on his side. "Leech's bar" became a State institution. It was open night and day for the whole eight years of his service. He said he found it cheaper than direct payment, and then he lumped all the costs in one item and had them paid by one appropriation bill, as "sundries." Why should he pay, he asked, for expenditures which were for the public benefit? And, indeed, why? As for himself, he boasted with great pride when the matter came up at a later time, that he never touched a drop. (IV, 340-41)

Page is more successful with those Northerners who are sympathetic to the South. His depiction of the Welch family has elicited praise from various critics who have felt that their favorable position in the novel clearly indicates Page's fairness to all the different types who settled in the post-war South;[4] but the Welches are really Southerners in disguise, and their immediate adoption of the Southern code of heroism simply reveals the author's bias. When Dr. Cary, as spokesman for the South, first asks Major Welch, "Do you expect to stay among us?" Welch understands what he means and asks in turn, "Do you mean, am I a carpet-bagger?" But Cary is serious, and he assures the Northerner, "I would not insult you under my roof by asking you that question. . . . I mean are you thinking of settling among us as a gentleman?" (IV, 467). The key word in this exchange is *gentleman,* and Welch knows what that word means. His next question refers to Hiram Still, and he wonders whether he can trust the scalawag. " 'Is he a gentleman?' interrupted Major Welch." And Cary answers: " 'Oh, no—certainly not that, sir. He is hand in glove with the carpetbaggers, and the leader of the negroes about here. He and a carpetbagger named Leech, and a negro preacher or exhorter named Sherwood, who, by the way, was one of my negroes, and a negro named Ash, who belonged to my friend General Legaie, and a sort of trick-doctor named Moses, whom I once saved from hanging, are the worst men in this section' " (IV, 468).

III *Reconstruction*

Character delineation is certainly not the most impressive aspect of Page's fiction, and in *Red Rock* he resorts consistently to sentimental stereotypes. What is impressive and far more successful in the novel is the panoramic vision of the prostrate

South. This view is not so objectively rendered as the author hoped it would be—all Radical Republicans and scalawags are automatically villainous, the insurgent Negroes are inevitably crude in their treachery; but the reader can find here, in dramatic terms, the clearest and most elaborate fictional description of Reconstruction from the Southern point of view. One senses Page's attempt to be disinterested—the prose often has great restraint, almost a "historical" flavor—as he tells the reader that "The absence of all civil government and the disorganization of the plantations were producing great inconvenience. Much thieving was going on everywhere, and there was beginning to be an unwonted amount of lawlessness: sheep and hogs were being stolen, and even horses and cattle" (IV, 225). But whenever Page becomes more specific and describes any of his characters closely, he loses firm control of his material. "'A nigger meetin' down yonder!" someone tells the military leaders. "'If it ain't broken up there'll be trouble. Leech started it by reading a paper he had, tellin' 'em the Gov'ment wants the party broke up, and then he put Sherrod up, and now that yaller nigger, Dr. Moses, is up. Leech's been givin' 'em liquor, and unless it's stopped there'll be the devil to pay'" (IV, 281).

There is constant movement from objectively rendered passages to those that are intensely subjective; as a consequence, the material of the novel is never clearly organized or well-defined, nor is the position of the novelist ever firmly established. The complexities of Reconstruction are avoided—the various political and financial motives of Radical Republicans were not so opportunistic and venal as Page suggests, the behavior of the Ku Klux Klan was by no means entirely retaliatory in nature, and the attitudes of whites toward the freedman were hardly as benevolent as they appear in this novel. Furthermore, the Negroes themselves were not so loyal to their past masters, nor were they so foolish and vulgar when they sought to vote.[5] The unfocused quality of the book is partially due to Page's desire to create a picture that "will stand for the South generally . . . rather than only for Virginia. The characters, perhaps, are more Virginian," he admitted to a friend, "than those of other States. . . . But then conditions, particularly those relating to the K.K.K. [are] such as prevailed in the more Southern States."[6]

In *Red Rock* Page avoids any real discussion of the poor-whites and the yeomen who formed a dominant force in the

South after the war; instead, he concentrates on the fallen plantation owner and his freedmen. There is no need to urge any special political position or even to censure him for his individual bias—that bias, after all, was as natural as that of a Radical Republican like Tourgée, who also sought objectivity in the account of his "fool's errand." All Reconstruction literature is polemical and politically tendentious in nature, and most of the literature dealing with race—even in the hands of present Negro and white writers—tends to dramatize attitudes that are too polarized and extreme. The point to be made, as well as the reason for the failure of *Red Rock,* is that Page's inability to admit the complexities of this period and the mixed motives of his characters makes the novel a superficial account of Reconstruction in which the South is a victim of Northern greed and all the actors of this drama are predictable types. This simplified version is evident in even those relatively objective passages of the book:

> Events had proved that although the people were impoverished, their spirit was not broken. Unhappily, the power was in the hands of those who did not understand them, and Leech and his fellows had their ear. It was deemed proper to put them in absolute control. Leech wrote the authorities that he and his party must have power to preserve the Union; he wrote to Mrs. Welch that they must have it to preserve the poor freedman. The authorities promised it, and kept the promise. It was insanity.
>
> One provision gave the ballot to the former slave, just as it was taken from the former master. An act was so shrewdly framed that, while it appeared simply to be intended to secure loyalty to the Union, it was aimed to strike from the rolls of citizenship almost the entire white population of the South; that is, all who would not swear they had never given aid or comfort to the Confederacy. It was so all-embracing that it came to be known as the "iron-clad" oath.
>
> "It is the greatest Revolution since the time of Poland," said Dr. Cary, his nostrils dilating with ire. "They have thrown down the man of intelligence, character, and property, and have set up the slave and the miscreant. 'Syria is confederate with Ephraim.' More is yet to come."
>
> "It is the salvation of the Union," wrote Leech to Mrs. Welch, who was the head of an organization that sent boxes of clothes to the negroes through Leech. Leech was beginning to think himself the Union. (IV, 324-25)

Such extreme opinions mar the historical sections of the book
and make the conflict between North and South seem almost
Manichean. Even more limited and biased is the specific description of the Negro voters themselves; it is like the bitter cartoon
that one finds in so many conservative newspapers of this period:

It was a strange sight, the polls guarded by soldiers; the men
who had controlled the country standing by, disfranchised, and
the lines of blacks who had just been slaves, and not one in one
hundred of whom could read their ballots, voting on questions
which were to decide the fate of the State. There were many
gibes flung at the new voters by the disfranchised spectators,
but they were mainly good-natured.

"Whom are you voting for Uncle Gideon?" asked Steve of one
of the old Red Rock negroes.

"Marse Steve, you know who I votin' for better'n I does
myself."

To another:

"Whom are you voting for?"

"Gi' me a little tobacker, Marse Steve, an' I'll tell you." And
when it was given, he turned to the crowd: "Who is I votin' for?
I done forgit. Oh! yes—old Mr. Linkum—ain' dat he name?"

"Well, he's a good one to vote for—he's dead," said Steve.

"Hi, is he? When did he die?" protested the old man in un-
feigned astonishment.

"You ain' votin' for him—you'se votin' for Mist' Grant," explained another younger negro, indignant at the old man's
ignorance.

"Is I? Who's he? He's one I ain' never heard on. Marse Steve,
I don' know who I votin' for—I jis know I votin', dat's all." (IV,
328-29)

This vision of black Reconstruction is similar to that of James
S. Pike in *The Prostrate State,* and it is clear that Page depends
on Pike, as well as on John A. Leland (in *A Voice from South
Carolina*), for his description of the corrupt politics of the
period. He acknowledges this debt in his letters to Arthur
Hobson Quinn and other contemporaries, and it is evident
throughout the middle sections of the book that the account of
the state assemblies, of voting processes and lawmaking, is
derivative and stereotypical. The reader never feels that the
author has personally witnessed what he is describing:

Assembly halls gave the majority an appearance of being overwhelming. They filled the porticos and vestibules, and thronged

the corridors and galleries in a dense mass, reveling in their newly acquired privileges. The air was heavy with the smoke of bad cigars, which, however, was not wholly without use, as the scent of the tobacco served at least one good purpose; the floors were slippery with tobacco-juice. The crowd was loud, pompous, and good-natured. Leech looked with curiosity on the curious spectacle. He had had no idea what a useful band of coadjutors he would have. He took a survey of the field and made his calculations quickly and with shrewdness. He would be a leader. (IV, 339)

IV *The Narrative*

The plot of *Red Rock,* perhaps the least significant element in the novel, involves the attempt of young Jacquelin Gray to regain possession of his family home. His father, as Dr. Cary reports to the visiting Northerner, Major Welch, "was killed at Shiloh, and his property all went to pay his debts afterward. He had some heavy indorsements, and it turned out that he owed a great deal of money to Still [the scalawag] for negroes he had bought to stock a large plantation he had in one of the other States—at least, the overseer gave this explanation, and produced the bonds, which proved to be genuine, though at first it was thought they must be forged. I suppose it was all right . . ." (IV, 465).

We follow the growth and development of Jacquelin Gray, who temporarily leaves the South for China (the reasons are not especially plausible, although Page tells us that the boy is weak and needs treatment in a special hospital there). When he returns, he is strengthened by his travels; he discovers that Hiram Still is the overseer in his father's house and that the land he had loved is tragically altered: "It was a great blow to Jacquelin to find on his return what extraordinary changes had taken place in the county: Still, occupying not only his old home, but Dr. Cary's; Leech the supreme power in all public matters in the county; Nicholas Ash driving a carriage, with money that must have been stolen; and almost the entire gentry of the State either turned out of their homes or just holding on, while those whom he had left half-amused children playing at the game of freedmen, were parading around the country in all the bravery and insolence of an armed mob" (IV, 421-22).

Jacquelin sets out to retrieve his family home, remembering

his father's last words: "Keep the old place. Make any sacrifice to do that. Landholding is one of the safeguards of a gentry. Our people, for six generations, have never sold an acre, and I never knew a man who sold land, that throve" (IV, 76). Of course, Jacquelin Gray succeeds—Still's bonds prove to be fraudulent—but only after a protracted suit that is interrupted by various excursions into Reconstruction politics, the workings of the Ku Klux Klan in Virginia, and Jacquelin's career in love. That career finds its consummation—but only after a number of rejections—in marriage to the Southern belle, Blair Cary.

The complementary love story is more interesting and thematically central to the novel: here, in the affair of Steve Allen and Ruth Welch, in the meeting of Southern hero and Northern lady, one witnesses once again the typical tale of reconciliation so popular in the literature of Reconstruction. This reconciliation joins the best of the two sections, and it fulfills the author's original intention never to write "a line which he did not hope might tend to bring about a better understanding between the North and the South, and finally lead to a more perfect Union" (I, xi). Through this love story and the conflict between the Welches and resistant Southerners, Page introduces whatever real dramatic conflict he has in the novel. The Welches dominate the second part of *Red Rock*, and it is clear that their increased presence is due to the author's realization that he has offered a very narrow view of intersectional conflict in Volume I.

Having presented the post-bellum South through the eyes of Southerners like Dr. Cary, Jacquelin Gray and Steve Allen, Page now attempts to gain distance and perspective by dramatizing the Welches' initial impressions of the South; but he selects their experiences and makes them as Southern as they can possibly be made—they see what he himself saw in the Reconstruction era. Their first experience is with a Negro insurrectionist, a freedman who actually demands his freedom. This is the type of Negro whom Page despises, and his description of the man is accordingly vulgar.

> He was a somewhat strongly-built, dark mulatto, perhaps a little past middle-age, of medium height, and . . . Ruth [Welch] thought she had never seen so grotesque a figure. . . . His chin stuck so far forward that the lower teeth were much outside of the upper, or, at least, the lower jaw was; for the teeth looked as though they had been ground down, and his gums, as he

grinned, showed as blue on the edge as if he had painted them. His nose was so short and the upper part of his face receded so much that the nostrils were unusually wide, and gave an appearance of a black circle in his yellow countenance. His forehead was so low that he had evidently shaved a band across it, and the band ran around over the top of his flat head, leaving a tuft of coarse hair right in the middle, and on either side of it were certain lines which looked as if they had been tattooed. (V, 6)

The Welches meet other unattractive figures of the South, such as Hiram Still and Jonadab Leech, and Page pictures the visiting Northerners as innocent victims of these unscrupulous people. Mrs. Welch is a representative of a Reform and Help Society, one of those many pious Northern ladies who came to the South during Reconstruction for idealistic purposes.[7] As soon as she demonstrates Republican attitudes and ceases to sympathize with the South, the community is no longer cordial to her and her family. And when she originates a school for Negro children without consulting the local residents, she meets with real antagonism. Negro schools were not objectionable to Southerners, according to Page, nor were they a novelty in the county—the Southern heroine, Blair Cary, had conducted one herself. "When, however, Mrs. Welch started her school, she consulted no one and asked no assistance—at least, of the country people. The aid she sought was only from her friends at the North, and when she received it, she set in, chose her place and built her school, giving out at the same time that [it] was to be used for sewing classes, debating societies, and other public purposes. Thus this school came to be considered as a foreign institution, conducted on foreign principles, and in opposition to the school already established by the neighborhood."[8]

This conflict, as real as it may seem when summarized, never results in true drama because Page always reports the differences between Northerners and Southerners but never shows them. As one Southerner says to Ruth Welch, "You aren't like them [Still and Leech]. You are more like us."

V *The Ku Klux Klan*

The novel grows coherent during its climax, when the Ku Klux Klan retaliates against the carpetbaggers, scalawags, and insurgent Negroes. Throughout the novel Page makes invidious comparisons between Leech and his white Southern victims, between debased, grotesque Negroes like Dr. Moses, who attempts to molest Ruth Welch, and the benevolent Mammy of Steve Allen, who warns Miss Welch, "Dat's my young master [Steve Allen]—my chile. . . . You're 'bliged to do what he say, you know" (V, 119). These extreme contrasts prepare the reader for the inevitable rise of the Klan so that when it does appear it can be seen as only defensive in nature.

The Klan that Page presents does not have unanimity of opinion. In the radical wing of the organization are those rabble rousers who use the organization to foment their own personal aggressions—these people, who were the rabid secessionists before the war, represent the worst elements of the South, and Page has little sympathy with them. Against the extremists he contrasts older conservatives like Dr. Cary and younger heirs of the best traditions of the South, people like Steve Allen and Jacquelin Gray. When the radical Klansmen want to hang Leech, Allen intercedes and urges moderation; and Jacquelin Gray even frees Leech from prison in the name of justice.

The Ku Klux Klan is never directly felt nor adequately presented. It emerges significantly in the last fourth of the novel, but not as a political force; the brutish Klansmen serve only to highlight the noble characteristics of true Southerners. Page is not so forceful nor so accurate as Albion W. Tourgée, that other fictional commentator on Reconstruction, for Page refuses to examine closely the more malevolent motives of many Klansmen. Whatever distortions are present in Tourgée's A Fool's Errand, his descriptions of the carpetbagger and Klansman succeed dramatically as Page's do not because the whole point of Tourgée's book is the exposure of the Klan and Southern militancy, Southern hostility—and this exposure is based upon Tourgée's own experiences in North Carolina. The tension between the Northern liberal and the Southern conservative is absent from Red Rock because both forces are finally heroic and in opposition to the seedier factions of North and South: the villains of this novel are the Leeches and the Stills and the McRaffles, who are Northern and Southern agitators. Politics yields to morality in Page's universe, and the significant distinction is between the gentleman and the boor, not between thoughtful Northerners and Southerners. "Gentlemen," Steve

Allen, the hero, announces, "are the same the world over in matters of honor" (V, 212).

The end of *Red Rock* suggests the moral burden that is carried by all of the author's characters. When Leech falls fatally ill, Dr. Cary attends him despite the corruption of the man and the doctor's opposition to him: "He has not money enough," Cary tells his wife, "the Governor has not money enough to induce me to go, if he were not ill. . . . I am going because he is sick and I am a physician" (V, 433). Upon curing Leech, Cary dies; the reader is given the impression of a saint-like man who has transcended personal bitterness. Dr. Cary, as Jacquelin Gray thinks of him, "seemed to be a part of the old life—in all the County, its best and most enduring type; and, now that he had gone, Jacquelin felt as though the foundation were falling out—as though the old life had passed away with him" (V, 435).

The act of greatest morality, however, is reserved for the hero, Steve Allen. Having abducted Leech from the Klansmen so that no bloodshed will occur, he surrenders himself to the Northern military and stands trial for his act. His courage is matched by his Northern lover, Ruth Welch, who, having witnessed Allen's abduction of Leech, agrees to marry him so that she cannot help to achieve his indictment. Ruth—as well as the Welch family and Steve Allen himself—is of course found innocent; and the mutual bravery of the Southern and Northern lovers is their defense against the political and social immorality of Leech, Still, and others who only want to make the South a land of spoils.

But Page concludes on a moral—not a political or social—note. This important point suggests why his version of Reconstruction is finally not an accurate one; it is not really concerned with the facts—not even with the facts as a point of departure for his special and narrow interpretation of the period. The judgments throughout the novel depend on the same distinctions he makes in his other fiction; there are gentlemen—Dr. Cary, Jacquelin Gray, Steve Allen, Major Welch—and there are those who have never learned, and consequently defy, the code of the gentleman. This rigid literary point of view, which may be suitable to the resurrection of a vanished glory, where analysis is not appropriate to fundamentally romantic materials, is extremely limited if not totally untenable in a novel concerned with the changes in a society and with the political conflicts inherent in those changes. This kind of novel is not compatible with Page's particular gifts—he himself recognized his limitations—and he inevitably resorts to the sentimental attitudes he finds easiest to manipulate and control.

His limitations can best be judged by juxtaposing his work with Tourgée's. In *A Fool's Errand* Tourgée comes to his material with the same literary point of view—he too has been indoctrinated with Scott and Cooper and other sentimental writers—but when he writes specifically about Reconstruction and the Ku Klux Klan and the insurgent Negro, he forgets his inherited attitudes and gives an accurate and powerful report; the reader passes over the sentimental love story and the moral platitudes for the historical crisis that lies within. In Page's book, however, sentimentality is so interfused with political strife that ultimately it dominates and shapes his subject matter. Both Tourgée and Page share identical literary and moral positions— but Tourgée had lived through Reconstruction as a judge and writer, a politician and active opponent of the Ku Klux Klan; the sense of personal contact with the period is absent from *Red Rock* and with it much of the dramatic power that should be in such a work.

VI *The End of a Dream*

Contemporary reviewers pointed out the obvious flaws of *Red Rock,* but many of them praised Page for his objectivity and fairness. Henry W. Lanier, son of the poet, noted the confused love affairs and excessive length of the novel; an English critic prefaced his comments by observing that "it is not as a story that [*Red Rock*] should be regarded, but rather as a picture of the Southern States after the war." Northern reviewers usually characterized the novel as literary propaganda but many were sympathetic to the author's views; *Red Rock,* wrote a critic for the *Atlantic Monthly,* is "good art if not exactly the best of realism. Mr. Page's sympathies are passionately Southern, and we have no doubt this fact colors his narrative to some extent." Similar reviews, which make invidious comparisons between the faulty artistry of *Red Rock* and the excellence of the early stories, appeared in contemporary periodicals.

Whatever its limitations, however, *Red Rock* achieved its political and literary purpose: it "cast a spell strong enough to exorcise Uncle Tom's ghost from all except the darkest, most benighted corners of the land."[9] The novel was considered by Page's friends and Southern sympathizers as the most effective literary refutation of *Uncle Tom's Cabin*.

To the modern reader *Red Rock*, from a technical point of view, is too long and sprawling, with no real form; and it is marred by prolixity and unnecessary digressions that have little to do with the point that Page is making. The lawsuit that forms the central strand of action is protracted endlessly and is of no real interest to the reader. What could be interesting—the conflict between the new freedmen and their former masters, the picture of the devastated South, the invasion of Carpetbaggers and Radical Republicans, the whole image of Black Reconstruction that is evoked by James Pike in *The Prostrate South*—becomes only confused because of the author's unwillingness to approach the materials realistically.

His attempt to write a more objective account than had yet been written, to defend the South against the slanders of *Uncle Tom's Cabin*, *A Fool's Errand*, and innumerable Northern newspaper reports, was exceptionally self-conscious and noteworthy, but he was not so impartial as early scholars and critics claimed.[10] Like all writers of Reconstruction literature, Page produced a political tract, whatever novelistic elements he uses; and the reasons are clear: he was too controlled by a belief in Negro inferiority and in the various intents of all carpetbaggers to see the end of the plantation system in truthful terms. His dream had ended—the dream that comprised most of his fiction until the writing of *Red Rock*, that filled all those stories of old Virginia for which he is known—and it is to his credit that he attempted to emerge from that dream into the real world of American literature and life. But Page was no novelist and he was no realist; and he did not have the necessary ability—one is tempted to use the word courage—to see the South in terms that were different from those he had always known and used.

CHAPTER *4*

Race

P AGE'S most comprehensive statement of race relations, *Red Rock*, marks the end of a certain nostalgia that he brought to his work. There are short excursions into old problems, and titles like "Bred in the Bone" (1901) and "Ole Jabe's Marital Experiment" (1902) suggest that he still used the Negro for fictional purposes; but he dealt fundamentally and seriously with these problems in the essay form, and in his fiction he searched for new themes. During this period—from 1898 until 1909, when he published *John Marvel, Assistant*—Page lived in Washington during the winters and occasionally visited his wife's cottage on Jekyl Isle, Georgia. In the summers the family went to York Harbor, Maine, where Page "formed many of the firm friendships of his life," friendships that found their way into some of the short tales of this period.

Most of his acquaintances were now wealthy Northerners or expatriate Southerners, and though he subsidized his home in Oakland, he rarely visited Virginia. His interests were elsewhere. He traveled to Europe and developed an attachment toward Italy, especially for the cities of Florence and Rome. At home in Washington, he became involved in national politics and helped Theodore Roosevelt in his election by successfully controlling much of the Virginia federal patronage. International politics commanded his attention, too, and when hostilities broke out in the Spanish-American War, he clearly announced his belief in white supremacy—especially in *The Coast of Bohemia*, a collection of poems, and in "The Dragon of the Seas," published in *The Washington Post* in 1898.[1] At the end of the Russo-Japanese War, Page joined Theodore Roosevelt, whose political views he shared throughout this period, in attempting to gain permanent legislation that would outlaw war. By this time he was a well-known figure in the social and political world of Washington. After the publication of *John Marvel* in 1909 he no longer wrote extensively, devoting almost all his time to politics and public affairs, and the few pieces he published were only echoes of older works.

The decade following *Red Rock* is characterized by a dimunition of quality in Page's short stories and novels and by the growth of power in his essays. His scattered stories, to be considered first, fall into two large groups: those dealing with race, and others that tend to be concerned with a new theme—the vanity of wealth—which now occupied his mind and found full expression in *Gordon Keith* (1903) and *John Marvel*. In the early 1900's he formulated most of his significant ideas on race in essays like "The Negro: The Southerner's Problem"; in this period he also wrote stories that pursue similar ideas, stories that lack the conviction and pathos of "Marse Chan" and "Meh Lady" but that nevertheless reassert his belief in heroism and white supremacy. Indeed, this belief becomes more pronounced, more mannered and rigid, as the stories deal less with specific historical events—myth takes over where history will no longer serve. The title of one of these stories suggests his position: "Bred in the Bone" was his favorite way of characterizing the proper relations of the races and of defining the superior traits of the Southern gentleman.

I *"Bred in the Bone"*

"Bred in the Bone" (1901), a story of horses, is a kind of updated, Virginian version of Lancelot and Guinevere. The central event is a steeplechase race in which the hero is tested before his lady; the central subject—the endless, tedious subject—is the pedigree of horses, or one is almost tempted to say, the racism of horses. "I know," an old trainer tells the young hero, "Dat's de blood! Imported Leamington—Fanny Wash'n' by Revenue! He'll do. Hit's bred in de bone!" (IX, 16). Page also asserts the supremacy of the rider who brings his own pedigree with him and is admired for it: "I never could understand," one member of his audience states, "why blood should count in horses and not in men."

At the race, with his young lady sitting prettily in the grandstand and cheering him, the hero loses the race; but he does so because he does not wish to injure his friend. The calculated defeat is more impressive than the victory he so easily could have achieved, and the reasons are simple: "Bone in muscle— and a green boy—with a pedigree" (IX, 54).

These years directly following the publication of *Red Rock* produced stories and poems with motives similar to that of "Bred in the Bone." The supremacy of the Anglo-Saxon race is evident in "The Dragon of the Seas," a poem Page published on April 5, 1898, in the *Washington Post*:

> They say the Spanish ships are out
> To seize the Spanish Main;
> Reach down the volume, Boy, and read
> The story o'er again:
>
> How when the Spaniard had the might,
> He drenched the Earth, like rain,
> With Saxon blood and made it Death
> To sail the Spanish Main.
>
> With torch and steel; with stake and rack
> He trampled out God's Truce
> Until Queen Bess her leashes slip't
> And let her sea-dogs loose.
>
> God! how they sprang and how they tore!
> The Gilberts, Hawkins, Drake!
> Remember, Boy, they were your sires:
> They made the Spaniard quake. (X, 237)

An even more direct statement of his belief in white supremacy is a ghost story, "The Spectre in the Cart," that he wrote a year later in 1899. The story is curiously macabre and grotesque and brutal; it is as if he had put aside literary convention for the moment and glimpsed into what might be the real future of racial tensions in the South. Told by a Southerner who scorns all belief in the supernatural, the anecdote involves two different men: Absalom Turnell, a Negro leader who stirs up other Negroes and directs them against whites; and John Halloway, a well-respected, resolute man who is a friend of the narrator. Halloway and his wife are murdered, and Turnell becomes the chief suspect. Page not only spoils his story by having the narrator preposterously dressed as a spectre who attempts to frighten Turnell into a confession, but he also offends the reader by describing the Negro as a traditionally superstitious buffoon. When the real murderer of Halloway confesses and hangs himself, a white mob assails Turnell and, in a strikingly brutal scene, lynches him. The whole story, a minor effort esthetically, is strangely direct and even crude in its hostile depiction of the Negro.

More typical of Page's literary attitudes is "Old Jabe's Marital Experiments" (1902). In it he recalls that period after the war when the Negroes were confused by their sudden freedom. Unlike the Negroes in the *Pastime Stories* or *Red Rock*, "Ole Jabe" is tenderly drawn; and though the point of view is obviously condescending, it is also affectionate. "Old Jabe's Marital Experiments," is one of Page's more successful character sketches, a portrait of a kindhearted but morally lax Negro who is reluctant to stay married too long to the same woman and who enjoys his freedom as well as the benefits of ante-bellum slavery: "Jabe's idea of emancipation was somewhat one-sided. He had all the privileges of a freedman, but lost none of a slave. He was free, but his master's condition remained unchanged: he still had to support him, when Jabez chose to call on him, and Jabez chose to call often. . . . 'Ef I don' come to you, who is I got to go to?' he demanded" (IX, 158).

His present wife dies and within two days he is already eying a white woman's cook. When the lady asks him why so many women marry him, the old man thinks for a moment and then answers: "Well I declar, 'mist'is, I hardly knows how. Dee wants to be fooled. I think it is becuz dee wants t' see what de urrs marry me fer, an' what dee done lef' me. Woman is might curisome folk" (IX, 167). It is clear, in a story like "Old Jabe's Marital Experiments," that Page was sincerely fond of the Negro, but only so long as the Negro remained a slave. His attitude is typical of many Southern authors of the post-bellum era: whatever understanding they bring to the colored man is controlled and modified by the Negro's willingness to perpetuate his role as slave.

This love for the faithful, reactionary Negro slave, before and after the war, is evident throughout Page's fiction. A good illustration of his technique in handling the post-bellum Negro who refuses his legal freedom is "Mam Lyddy's Recognition" (1904); in it he eulogizes a mammy, "a deep-dyed aristocrat": "Mam' Lyddy had been in the French family all her life, as her mother and grandmother had been before her. She had rocked on her ample bosom the best part of three generations. And when Freedom came, however much she may have appreciated being free, she had much too high an estimate of the standing of the Frenches to descend to the level of the class she had always condemned as 'free niggers.' She was a deep-dyed aristocrat" (IX, 219-20).

The conflict of the story is between Lyddy and other Negroes who assert their freedom. Lyddy's mistress Betty French complains to her husband about the other domestic help: "I do not know what is the matter . . . I always thought I could get along with colored people; but somehow these are different. . . ." "Spoiled," her husband answers. "The mistake was in the emancipation proclamation. *Domestic* servants ought to have been excepted" (IX, 228). Mam' Lyddy remains loyal until she is infected by the new ideas and wants to join "the Colored Ladies Society Club" and until she asks for the money she earns from the French people so that she can invest it herself. But, confronted by her master and mistress, she obviously does not know what she wants:

> "I want *rec'nition.*"
> "Want recognition? What do you mean?"
> "Dat's what *we* wants," declared the old woman, acquiring courage.
> Graeme [her master] laughed.
> "What is recognition?"
> "I don't know what 't is edzac'ly, but dat's what we *wants.* You all 's got it and got to gi' it to *us.*"
> "You mean you want to sit at table with us?" exclaimed Mrs. Graeme.
> Mammy Lyddy turned toward her. "You know I don't mean nuttin' like that! I leetle more'n smacked that yaller gal' what you call you' maid over 'bout talkin' dat way t' other day."
> "Then what do you want?"
> "I wants *rec'nition*—dat's all I wants." (IX, 241-42)

The point, of course, is that Mam Lyddy is not ready for freedom, for self-government; she is essentially a child who still needs the paternal and maternal advice of her old owners. She has been given these rebellious notions by a fraudulent minister who only intends to fleece her of her money. When she discovers his malicious intentions, she no longer wants "recognition"—she wants her money: "I wants to git hold of dat black nigger what 's done rob me, talkin' 'bout bein' sich a friend o' Caesar's." Graeme asks her, "Do you want to go home"; and she answers, "Dis is my home." She has been "converted," as Mrs. Graeme says; and she utters those words which are the great wish-fulfillment of Page's sympathetic characters: "It is like old times" (IX, 252).

By this point in his career, Page no longer attempts to be original in the use of traditional materials; he employs the same framework for his stories, and he does not infuse them with spontaneity or freshness; the reader senses the indifference of the author himself. In "The Christmas Peace" (1904), he repeats the traditional motive of the two feuding families and their consequent victimization of the lovers; the lovers marry and with their son finally succeed in harmonizing the feelings of all family members. "A Soldier of the Empire" does not deal with the South, but the motives are identical to those of the Southern stories—"A Soldier of the Empire" contains all the basic characteristics that he brought to literature. "It was his greatest pride in life," Page writes, "that he had been a soldier—a soldier of the empire. He was known simply as 'The Soldier,' and it is probable that there was not a child in the Quarter who did not know him: the tall, erect old Sergeant with his white, carefully waxed moustache, and his face seamed with two sabre cuts. One of these cuts, all knew, had been received the summer day when he had stood, a mere boy, in the hollow square at Waterloo, striving to stay the fierce flood of the 'men on the white horses' " (IX, 307).

So the hero is presented; now he is defending the glory of France. As in all of Page's fiction, there is no irony, no sublety: heroism is the abstraction the reader must accept in order to have any appreciation for the story that follows. That story is indeed simple: the old sergeant has a son, Pierre, who is a deserter; the father, in shame, intends to shoot him; but when the enemy kills the boy, the father goes on to fight bravely and dies heroically:

> A second [man], looking at the body of an old French sergeant amidst heaps of slain, with his face to the sky, said simply as he saw his scars:
> "There died a brave soldier."
> Another, older than the first, bending closer to count the

bayonet wounds, caught the gleam of something in the light of the lantern, and stooping to examine a broken cross of the Legion on the dead man's breast, said reverently:
"He was a *soldier of the empire.*" (IX, 333-34)

The point of the story—if there is any point beyond another description of heroism—is that the younger generation cannot function like the older, that they are weaker and more feeble and more cowardly. In any case, it is interesting to note that the people who murmur the eulogy over the "soldier of the empire" are with "a group of Prussian officers." Page presents the military conflict between France and Germany as he presented the conflict between North and South, suggesting that heroism knows no nationality. Within fifty years these same two countries were engaged in another bitter conflict, which involved his own country. Within twenty years after the publication of "The Soldier of the Empire," Americans began their skeptical exploration of heroism, their denial of all those abstractions like honor and glory that Page finds so congenial. In this generation of more cynical and bitter writers, Hemingway stated for a whole group of disillusioned soldiers—although soldiers of no empire—that words like *honor* and *hallow* were obscene beside the concrete names of villages, the numbers of streets.

Page, who died in 1922, saw his point of view become obsolete in his own lifetime. Even at the time he published "A Soldier of the Empire" and other stories like "Bred in the Bone" and "Mam Lyddy's Recognition" he was out of date with the literature written by his significant contemporaries. William Dean Howells had created *A Modern Instance* in 1881 and *A Hazard of New Fortunes* in 1890; Stephen Crane had written *Maggie, A Girl of the Street* in 1893; and authors such as Theodore Dreiser, Frank Norris, Henry Fuller, and Harold Frederic were pointing to a more realistic approach to life and literature. Page was not only out of step with the literary currents of his own time but with the racial and political ones as well. He did not really respond to the New South that Henry Grady had helped to inaugurate; Page claimed that "the New South is in my judgment only the Old South with Slavery gone and the fire of exaction on its back."[2] And, of course, his solution to racial matters was very different from that of George

Washington Cable and other liberal Southerners. The view that social status and breeding were "in the bone" was as antiquated as the code of heroism he automatically gave his Southern gentlemen.

II *Other Literary Types*

Page was primarily a short story writer, although he attempted other types of literature such as drama and poetry, the novel and the essay. His interest in drama began in 1892 when he submitted "a Southern play" to Augustin Daly, a producer; but Daly was not impressed by the manuscript. Several years later he tried to interest the actor Sol Smith Russell in a drama entitled *In Ole Virginia*; but Russell thought that it was not "in its present form a good acting play—the character drawing is too fragmentary. They come too much in bits or suggestions and there are no scenes of strength. . . . The one purpose indicated being to show a phase of southern life now gone bye [*sic*] your play needs a stronger backbone than this."[3] In 1900 he collaborated with another aspiring dramatist, George Clarke, but the play that they had agreed to write was soon abandoned. He turned to an attempted dramatization of *Red Rock*; but no producer would handle the finished play.

The only published drama of his career was *The Hostage, or Along the Potomac: A One Act Play* (1906) in which a Northern colonel is imprisoned by a Southern major for stealing horses. Page attempts to create local color by introducing Negro slaves— one Caroline, who is loyal to her master, the Southern major; and her son Zeke, who is lazy and wants his freedom. These minor characters—stereotypes with which readers of Page are familiar—are the most vivid characters in the play. The white figures tediously express their desire for reconciliation. Page was not suited to be a dramatist, for it was difficult for him to create through dialogue the nostalgia, the background, the local color necessary for a successful re-creation of the past.

His poetry is not successful either. "Uncle Gabe's White Folks," his first published poem, appeared in *Scribner's Monthly* in April, 1877. It is one of a number of dialect poems—"Little Jack," "Ashcake," "Zekyl's Infidelity," "Marse Phil"—that were to follow; these poems are similar in technique and point of view to the more successful, more controlled stories of *In Ole Virginia*. They are fundamentally evocations, and they assert not only the fraternalism of Negro and white but also the inherent racial superiority of the white man:

> You' gran'pa bought my mammy at Gen'l Nelson's sale,
>   An' Deely she come out de same estate;
> An' blood is jes' like pra'r is—hit tain' gwine nuver fail;
>   Hit's sutney gwine to come out, soon or late.
>
> When I wuz born, yo' gran'pa gi' me to young Marse Phil,
>   To be his body-servant—like, you know;
> An' we growed up together like two stalks in a hill—
>   Bofe tarslin' an' den shootin' in de row.
>
> Marse Phil wuz born in harves', an' I dat Christmas come;
>   My mammy nussed bofe on we de same time;
> No matter what one got, suh, de oder gwin git some—
>   We wuz two fibe-cent pieces in one dime. (X, 306-7)

More traditional in nature are those poems Page included in *The Coast of Bohemia* (1906). These uninspired pieces tend to be sentimental and are no different from the popular verse one finds in most journalism of the period. There are religious lyrics —"The Needle's Eye," "The Closed Door," "Convention," "The Magdalen," "The Requirement"—that offer conventional tributes to God. Love poems like "The Stranger," "Love," "An Old Refrain," "To Claudia," resemble Poe's verse; but, in spite of the formal correctness, the passion and lyric sweep are absent:

> It is not, Claudia, that thine eyes
>   Are sweeter far to me,
> Than is the light of Summer skies
>   To captives just set free. (X, 268)

Page attempts to elevate the language of these poems by using a biblical phraseology, but his gestures to the dawn, to his mother, or to the sea remain traditional ones traditionally rendered. The only theme that distinguishes the verse of *The Coast of Bohemia,* that might stamp the verse as distinctly Page's, is the familiar attitude toward heroism. The keynote is struck in the title poem:

> There rest the heroes of lost causes lorn
> On their calm brows more fadeless chaplets far
> Than all their conquerors' could e'er adorn,

When shone ascendant Fame's effulgent star;
There fallen patriots reap the glorious prize
Of deathless memory of their precious sacrifice. (X, 214)

The verse continues in this vein, replete with capitalized abstractions—*Love* and *Sorrow* and *Joy* and *Honor*—and with predictable attitudes that attend them. There is no subtlety to his poetic sensibility, and the poems that he wrote are undistinguished and ephemeral in their traditional sentimentality. They are "the product of a love for poetry" rather than "a great necessity for utterance."[4] He recognized his own limitations in a preface to the original edition: "there is for the minor poet," he wrote, "also a music that the outer world does not catch—an inner day which the outer world does not see. It is this music, this light which, for the most part, is for the lesser poet his only reward that he has heard, however brokenly, and at however vast a distance, snatches of those strains which thrilled the souls of Marlowe and Milton and Keats and Shelley, even though he may never reproduce one of them, is moreover a sufficiently high reward."[5]

III *White Supremacy*

More important than Page's excursions into drama and poetry, and more representative of his basic attitudes, is a second series of essays that he wrote from 1901 through 1907 and collected in two volumes: *The Negro: The Southerner's Problem* (1904) and *The Old Dominion: Her Making and Her Manners* (1907). The first of these books is of special significance and continues the argument Page first outlined in "The Race Question" (1892). More than any other single work it represents, as Edmund Wilson has remarked, his "attempt to deal frankly with the harassing problems,"[6] and it remains today as one of the classic definitions of a Southern view of the Negro.

Page begins by noting how divergent the views of the two sections are, "the one [the North] esteeming the question to be merely as to the legal equality of the races, and the other passionately holding it to be a matter that goes to the very foundations of race-domination and race integrity."[7] He reiterates his central thesis that Northerners simply do not understand the Negro. In order to dramatize the confusion that has resulted from the Northerner's treatment of racial problems, he recalls the loyalty that existed between slave and master before and during the Civil War. "Many a master going to the war intrusted his wife and children to the care of his servants with as much confidence as if they had been of his own blood. They acted rather like clansmen than like bondmen" (22). The war succeeded in bringing Negroes and whites of the South closer together; and when it was over, "the friendship between the races was never stronger; the relations were never more closely welded" (25). He concludes his first chapter, entitled "Slavery and the Old Relation Between the Southern Whites and Blacks," by once again characterizing, in lyrical fashion, the intimacy of white and black in the old South:

> The entire generation which grew up during and just after the war grew up with the young Negroes, and preserved for them the feeling and sympathy which their fathers had had before them. This feeling may hardly be explained to those who have not known it. Those who have known it will need no explanation. It possibly partakes somewhat of a feudal instinct; possibly of a clan instinct. It is not mere affection; for it may exist where affection has perished and even where its object is personally detested. Whatever it is, it exists universally with those who came of the slave-holding class in the South, who knew in their youth the Negroes who belonged to their family, and, no matter what the provocation, they can no more divest themselves of it than they can of any other principle in their lives. (27-28)

Having presented this period when relations between the races were so harmonious, Page now discusses "what changes have taken place since that time" (29). The point he wishes to make—the one implied in the title and repeated throughout the book—is that racial relations have declined because those who do not understand the Negro have tried to legislate him into a state of equality. As far as Page is concerned, "the position of the South on these points is sound; that, however individuals of one race may appear the equals of individuals of the other race, the races themselves are essentially unequal" (32). The errors committed by the North since the Civil War have been legion. He attacks the Freedmen's Bureau for assuming "that the interest of the blacks and of the whites were necessarily opposed to each other, and that the blacks needed protection against the whites in all cases" (35); he criticizes the Northerner for disregarding the "statement of any Southern white person, however pure in life, lofty in morals, high-minded in principle he might be" (36); he scolds "the new missionaries" who went counter to the deepest prejudice of the Southern people because "they lived with the Negroes, consorting with them, and appearing with them on terms of apparent intimacy" (38-39); he denounces the Union League, claiming that their "meetings were held at night, with closed doors, and with pickets guarding the approaches, and were generally under the direction of the most hostile members of the Freedmen's Bureau" (39). And of course he laments the role of the carpetbaggers: "No sooner had the Southern armies laid down their guns and the great armies of the North who had saved the Union disbanded, than the vultures, who had been waiting in the secure distance, gathered to the feast" (40).

His version is the standard Southern interpretation of Reconstruction, and one can find its dramatization in *Red Rock*. But one should note, as a corrective to some of Page's extreme views, that the Freedmen's Bureau was not nearly so prejudiced toward Southern whites—a point that a perusal of John W. De Forest's *A Union Officer in the Reconstruction* illustrates. It is true that, in general, Radical Republicans did not heed sufficiently the views of the intelligent Southern whites, and it is also true that Northern missionaries sympathized with the Negroes in defiance of Southern attitudes—Tourgée's *A Fool's Errand* (1879) and *Bricks Without Straw* (1880) dramatize both these points. But Tourgée—a leading Northern commentator on Reconstruction in the South, a judge, and a carpetbagger who came to North Carolina and stayed there until 1879—helped to originate the Union League, and it was not nearly so militant as Page claims. Furthermore, Tourgée represents one of many carpetbaggers who had not waited "in the secure distance" during the war and who were not simply "vultures . . . gathered to the feast."

The victim of Reconstruction, according to Page, was the Negro. Like Joel Chandler Harris (in *Gabriel Tolliver*) and Thomas Dixon (in *The Clansman, The Leopard's Spots,* and *The Traitor*), Page brings to his comments on the Negro a pious condescension that is bitterly ironic in the glare of twentieth-century American history:

> However high the motive may have been, no greater error could have been committed; nothing could have been more

disastrous to the Negro's future than the teaching he thus received. He was taught that the white man was his enemy when he should have been taught to cultivate his friendship. He was told he was the equal of the white when he was not the equal; he was given to understand that he was the ward of the nation when he should have been trained in self-reliance; he was led to believe that the Government would sustain him when he could not be sustained. In legislation, he was taught thieving; in politics, he was taught not to think for himself, but to follow slavishly his leaders (and such leaders!); in private life, he was taught insolence. A laborer, dependent on his labor, no greater misfortune could have befallen him than estrangement from the Southern whites. To instil into his mind the belief that the Southern white was his enemy; that his interest was necessarily opposed to that of the white, and that he must thwart the white man to the utmost of his power, was to deprive him of his best friend and to array against him his strongest enemy. (47-48)

The proper relation of the races, he concludes, is that of master and servant; for, whenever the "instigation of Northerners" was removed, the Negroes "were ready to resume their old relation of dependence and affection" (51).

That the only good Negro is the servile or abject one is advanced in a third chapter, "Its [the Negro Problem's] Present Condition and Aspect, as Shown by Statistics." In it Page concentrates on what he believes is Negro inferiority. He admits that slavery was "the greatest evil that ever befell this country," but only because "it kept the sections divided and finally plunged the nation into a devastating civil war." As for the Negro himself, "it was far from an unmixed evil. This very period of slavery in America had given to him the only semblance of civilization which the Negro race has possessed since the dawn of history" (57). Since the days of slavery, the Negroes have risen only in those regions where they "have had the aid, sympathy, and encouragement of the whites" (75). Left alone, the post-bellum Negro has not demonstrated a capacity to elevate himself:

> Universally, they will tell you that while the old-time Negroes were industrious, saving, and, when not misled, well-behaved, kindly, respectful, and self-respecting, and while the remnant of them who remain still retain generally these characteristics, the "new issue," for the most part, are lazy, thriftless, intemperate,

insolent, dishonest, and without the most rudimentary elements of morality.

They unite further in the opinion that education such as they receive in the public schools, so far from appearing to uplift them, appears to be without any appreciable beneficial effect upon their morals or their standing as citizens. But more than this; universally, they report a general depravity and retrogression of the Negroes at large in sections in which they are left to themselves, closely resembling a reversion to barbarism. (80)

This reversion to barbarism is exhibited in the Negro's sexuality. Page uses as evidence the comments of a Northern Negro who in *The American Negro* writes of the "moral lapses" of his race:

"All who know the Negro recognize, however, that the chief and overpowering element in his make-up is an imperious sexual impulse which, aroused at the slightest incentive, sweeps aside all restraints in the pursuit of physical gratification. We may say now that this element of Negro character constitutes the main incitement to degeneracy of the race and is the chief hindrance to its social up-lifting. . . .

"The Negro's ethical code sternly reprobates dancing, theatre attendance, and all social games of chance. It does not, however, forbid lying, rum-drinking, or stealing. Furthermore, a man may trail his loathsome form into the sanctity of private homes, seduce a wife, sister, or daughter with impunity, and be the father of a score of illegitimate children by as many mothers, and yet be a disciple of holiness and honored with public confidence." (82-83)

Because of the rather rambling, impressionistic evidence that Page has marshalled in support of the Negro's depravity, the reader is prepared for his comments on lynching. Though lynching "as a remedy" to the race problem has been "a ghastly failure," though "its brutalizing effect on the community is incalculable" (109), white Southerners have resorted to it for only defensive reasons: "the Negro does not generally believe in the virtue of women. It is beyond his experience. He does not generally believe in the existence of actual assault. It is beyond his comprehension. In the next place, his passion, always his controlling force, is now, since the new teaching, for the white women" (112).

Page seeks the solution to Negro brutality (it is curious, incidentally, that he alludes only briefly to the white man's ravaging of Negro women). Separation of the races and colonization are no longer feasible, for the Negroes have increased from less than a million at the beginning of the nineteenth century to nine millions in 1900. Furthermore, he admits, "the Negroes have rights; many of them are estimable citizens; and even the great body of them when well regulated, are valuable laborers" (107-8). Lynching is no solution either, for it "does not end ravishing, and that is the prime necessity." The only possible answer to racial strife and brutality is the creation of "a sound public opinion which, instead of fostering, shall reprobate and sternly repress the crime of assaulting women and children. . . . Lynching will never be done away with while the sympathy of the whites is with the lynchers, and no more will ravishing be done away with while the sympathy of the Negroes is with the ravisher. When the Negroes shall stop applying all their energies to harboring and exculpating Negroes, no matter what their crime may be so it be against the whites, and shall distinguish between the law-abiding Negro and the lawbreaker, a long step will have been taken" (115-16).

The burden of moral responsibility should be placed on Negro leaders. Page, who admires Booker T. Washington, William Hannibal Thomas, and Bishop Turner, is convinced that "few ravishings by Negroes would occur if the more influential members of the race were charged with responsibilities for the good order of their race in every community" (118-19). He amplifies upon these ideas in other essays that he included in *The Negro: the Southerner's Problem*. In "The Partial Disfranchisement of the Negro," he urges "the politician and the doctrinaire"—that is, Northerners—to "hold hands off. The best service the Negro's best friend can render him is to tell him the truth. The direst injury the Negro's worst enemy can do him is to perpetuate hostility between him and the Southern White. Left to themselves they would settle the question along economic lines, and this it must come to at last" (162). In "The Old-Time Negro," he recalls fondly the hierarchy of Negroes—house servants, field hands, assistant superintendants—and emphasizes that the Negroes' family ties "often appear to be scarcely as strong now as they were under the institution of slavery." With the loss of plantation life, the Negro lost a grip on his moral nature. His own family relations have deteriorated; marital infidelity has become more pronounced; and husbands desert their children and act like animals.

The Negro's present immorality is sharply juxtaposed with his role in ante-bellum times when he had grandeur and respect (although he never transgressed his contented role of servant), when he was indeed more educated than most people realized, and when he chose not only to go to war with his master as a body servant but to remain a servant in the Reconstruction period. Those who left the plantations after the war were ungrateful Negroes who had always been troublesome. As conclusive evidence, he cites two of the servants who worked on his plantation: Ralph, who was his father's body servant; and old Hannah, his mother's maid.

Ralph had fought by his master's side in the Civil War, and their mutual loyalty had been intense. Their return from the War, as described by the author, takes on the lyric proportions, the climactic and sentimental overtones, of a great drama—one sees the scene and imagines innumerable other scenes like it throughout the South. For a twelve-year-old boy to witness this homecoming—his father's desecration and defeat, the fall of a civilization that had always seemed immense and impenetrable—was indeed as traumatic as the loss of innocence, the awareness of original sin: "I remember the way in which, as he slipped from his horse, he put his hand over his face to hide his tears, and his groan, 'I never expected to come home so.' All were weeping. A few minutes later he came out on the porch and said: 'Ralph, you are free; take the saddles off and turn the horses out'" (192). The second scene involves Hannah, the maid of his mother:

> . . . after the war, as before it, [Hannah] served us with a fidelity and zeal of which I can give no conception. It may, however, illustrate it to state that, although she lived a mile and a quarter from the house and had to cross a creek, through which, in time of high water, she occasionally had to wade almost to her waist, she for thirty years did not miss being at her post in the morning more than a half-score times.
>
> Hannah has gone to her long home, and it may throw some light on the old relation between mistress and servant to say that on the occasion of the golden wedding of her old master and mistress, as Hannah was at that time too ill to leave her

home, they took all the presents in the carriage and carried them over to show them to her. Indeed, Hannah's last thought was of her old mistress. She died suddenly one morning, and just before her death she said to her husband, 'Open the do', it's Miss——.' The door was opened, but the mistress was not there, except to Hannah's dying gaze. To her, she was standing by her bedside, and her last words were addressed to her. (201-2)

Thus dies the myth of beneficent slavery, of healthy relations between mistress and servant. Page's superior attitudes toward the Negro, his absolute commitment to Negro inferiority, is shared openly by only the most militant racists in the country today. Tacit agreement is, however, widespread; and white people have not advanced, in many practical ways, very far beyond their ancestors at the turn of the century. Historically, Page's essay represents a position that can be traced throughout the nineteenth century in the writings of John P. Kennedy, John Esten Cooke, William Caruthers, William Gilmore Simms, and many others; it is the apotheosis of that reactionary attitude, and it is mirrored in the tales of Joel Chandler Harris and the less effective fiction of Thomas Dixon. Since Page's time, the class distinctions are perhaps not so clearly drawn, and there is an attempt—in the fiction of Ellen Glasgow, for example—to describe the Negro as a human being. But too often the Negro represents an idea or an abstraction that the writer is promulgating; and this judgment holds true for the Negro as well as the white writer. In any historical account of the white man's relation to the Negro, *The Negro: the Southerner's Problem* should be of particular importance; for it illuminates a position widely held in Page's own time, one that is not so outdated as may at first appear. That position must be understood before the problems of racial relations can be solved, and Page's essay is a good beginning.

IV *Manners, Morals, and Customs of the South*

Less tendentious and more discursive in its treatment of Southern customs is a second volume of essays, *The Old Dominion: Her Making and Her Manners* (1907). Like the first series of lectures and articles collected in *The Old South,* these commentaries on Southern life are concerned with social status and pedigree; once again manners and morals—fused into what we have seen is a code of social heroism—are of central significance.

History—and especially Southern history—was always an absorbing subject for Page, and one finds a high seriousness and a respect in this writing that are not present in much of his fiction of the same period. He begins with the discovery of America; and, as he traces the well-known events of settlement in Colonial America, the events turn in almost every instance upon the courage of some individual hero. Columbus, Drake, Raleigh—these are the adventurers whom Page sees in purely romantic terms, and he adopts without question those familiar anecdotes that have been associated with their names.

With the tributes offered to certain well-known heroes, Page also commends the pioneers who first settled in the country. They established the Anglo-Saxon race at Jamestown, he writes with pride; "three hundred years ago, on this small island in this Virginia river, that little band of sea-worn adventurers disembarked and planted the flag of the Anglo-Saxon race, which, though often threatened, and sometimes endangered, has never since been lowered" (XIII, 91). Racial distinctions are firmly made and fostered at the outset, and there is an automatic association between heroism or supremacy and the Anglo Saxon race. This association, from Page's point of view, goes beyond analysis and offers the terms with which he presents all racial conflicts in Southern history. The original courage and the individualism of the pioneers are exemplary, he writes; they are characteristics of a golden age of heroic endeavor. What has passed with that age is the romantic quality of wonder:

> Our imagination has been almost destroyed by the destruction of the standards by which we form our conceptions. The wonders of the world are scarcely any longer wonderful, and the labors of Hercules are excelled by the work of thousands of enterprising companies every day of our life. We may now coast for pleasure where three hundred years ago it was more dangerous to venture than to beard the Nemean lion roused. The vast *terra incognita* that stretched illimitably before the eager eyes of those settlers is as familiar to us as a city park to the inhabitants about it; and the trackless wild, which seemed to swallow them up, is a part of the habitual round of the pleasure-travelling public. But on that May day three hundred years ago, when the company

of those little ships debarked and made their final landing on American soil, they faced every peril and danger that the human mind can imagine. (XIII, 94-95)

This nostalgia is traditional on the part of the author, and one might suspect that in these essays on colonial life he is guilty of distortion; but he strains for objectivity and in general is successful because he is not so defensive or apologetic as he is in *The Negro: the Southerner's Problem.* In *The Old Dominion* he has no serious commitment to any one position, and the style is more relaxed and ingratiating, less cluttered by offensive posturing. Furthermore, the sincere affection in his appraisal of these early settlers reflects his generous temperament. But he is not a historian and these essays are not history; they are romantic recollections of the glory of America. And herein lie their value for any study of Page's work or the literary history of the South; the point of view, in not being extreme, is an index to the thought of most nineteenth-century Southerners.

Page traces the development of manners throughout the eighteenth century and discusses that time during which the

gentry lived upon their great estates, working their tobacco, managing their slaves and the affairs of the colony; breeding their fine horses, and racing them in good old English style; asserting and maintaining their privileges; visiting and receiving visits; marrying and giving in marriage; their wives rolling about in their coaches-and-four, dressed in satins and brocades brought in their own ships from London; their daughters in fine raiment, often made by their own hands ("Journal of a Young Lady of Virginia"), dancing, reading, and marrying; vying with their husbands and lovers in patriotism; sealing up their tea, and giving up all silk from England except for hats and bonnets (a charming touch); their sons going to William and Mary or across to Oxford or Cambridge, and growing up like their sires, gay, pleasure-loving, winning and losing garters on wagers, jealous of privilege, proud, assertive of their rights, ready to fight and stake all on a point of principle, and forming that society which was the virile soil from which sprang this nation. (XII, 142-43)

Now the nostalgic chauvinism, so sentimentally rhapsodic in its recounting of this peaceful period, is closer to the author's own real interests; he places the roots of American heroism firmly in eighteenth-century Virginia. And as he cites the names of Washington and Jefferson, he speaks with a pride that can be respected. He draws the reader's attention to the significant role that early Virginians played in the formulation of the basic principles of the nation. In speaking of "The Revolutionary Movement," for example, he writes dispassionately and persuasively when he considers basic history, when he informs us that the Stamp Act joined colonists together; but the moment he turns to Virginia's role in the Revolution he is inevitably involved in the writing of hagiography. His comments on Washington are a good example of this type of tribute:

> It is still easy, after a hundred and thirty years, to distinguish him from all the rest. Sprung from Virginia's soil, compact of the elements that have given distinction to the character that bears her stamp; country bred; level-headed rather than clever; direct and straightforward rather than astute or keen; inspired by her traditions; tempered on the anvil of adversity to be the truest instrument that Providence had ever fashioned to its hand; following with divine patience and divine humility the call of duty, that lordly Virginian rides down the years, still easily distinguished from all the rest. And the only one [Thomas Jefferson] of all the company who bears a close resemblance to him was, like him, a Virginian also. (XIII, 177)

Thomas Jefferson is the other hero of old Virginia. Page considers Jefferson's desire to educate all Southerners in his establishment of the University of Virginia; for fifty years Jefferson had thought of this project, and for twenty years he gave it his energies. And from its conception, it became an institution highly regarded throughout the nation: "Students were drawn there from all over the country, though mainly, as Jefferson had foretold, from the South and West, and there is not a State in that section which has not felt in every profession the vivifying effects of its teachings. Bench and bar, pulpit and medical faculty have all been uplifted by the high standard set in the University of Virginia. Here Poe drew his inspiration for those immortal works which have made him the first poet and first story-writer of America. And here many less noted, but not less worthy sons have found the equipment with which they have served their age and country" (XIII, 228-29).

These essays concerning Colonial Virginia are symptomatic of

Page's romantic attitude toward history. But as chauvinistic as he may be, as extravagant as his defense of local customs and manners may seem at times, there is an eloquence and quiet charm throughout these recollections that are particularly suited to their subject.

Other essays present a later picture of Virginian life and offer a more detached view, describing the life of eighteenth- and nineteenth-century Virginia in a quiet and infectious manner. In "An Old Virginia Sunday" (1901), he returns to his small area in Hanover County where "only one gentleman in the country had ever crossed the ocean" and "the solitary mail-rider passed up the road twice a week" (XIII, 344). In the lives of the provincial people, religion was a vital element—"it gave the complexion to their life, and with chivalry and love of the rights of freemen, gave its fibre" (XIII, 376). Their piety was almost as great as that of the Puritans; the "one man in the neighborhood who was openly an unbeliever . . . was looked on . . . with somewhat the same awe with which a man condemned to death is regarded."

The religious spirit so present in early nineteenth-century Virginia ought to be emphasized. Although Page himself had no serious commitment to formal religion, there is a moral urgency throughout his writings that clearly stems from this early period in his life. His comments on the reading habits of those people who influenced him suggest why his own moral attitudes were so strong and inflexible:

> Our reading was carefully looked after and guarded, all our "week-day books" being prohibited and our reading being confined to "Sunday books." Prominent among these were Mrs. Sherwood's works, beginning with "Henry Milner," "Little Henry and His Bearer," and "The Fairchild Family," the latter a grim and terrifying collection of moral teachings. One of these I well remember was an account of an excursion on which the father took little Harry and Lucy, after a quarrel, to see hanging on a gibbet the body of a man who had killed his brother.
> The writer was nearly thirty years old before he ever saw a lady read a novel on Sunday, and such is the effect of early training that he never sees one so engaged now without its raising doubts, at least, as to her social standing. (XIII, 386)

Two other essays in this series of commentaries on Southern history and customs bring Page closer to the period during which he lived. In "The Southern People During Reconstruction" and in "The Old Dominion Since the War" he is unnecessarily defensive and excessively chauvinistic—as he always tends to be in discussing racial tensions. When he speaks of the Southerners' attitude toward the war, he emphasizes the large number of conservatives—especially in Virginia—who did not want to fight in the Civil War but who "could not tolerate invasion"; these men left for the war and returned from it "with a belief that they were unconquerable." Indeed, it is sometimes difficult in reading these essays to determine who won the Civil War. Turning to Reconstruction, Page is predictable in his attitudes: he blames the Freedmen's Bureau, Radical Reconstructionists, and Andrew Johnson; he deplores Black Reconstruction and the dominion of the Negroes, whom he considers to be the innocent dupes of the Radical Republicans.

Sectional chauvinism is more evident in "The Old Dominion Since the War." Though Virginia is poor in the post-bellum period, Page warns the reader that "the want of money is not poverty, and the old age [of the state] is not decrepitude" (XIII, 293). He has a good deal to say here and throughout his essays and fiction on the basic distinction between money and pedigree. Wealth means "absolutely nothing" to the Virginian, for the heroic individual can always make money; his chief glory is that he is Virginian. It may be true, as Lionel Trilling has suggested, that the masterpieces of American literature— *Moby Dick, The Scarlet Letter*—are not primarily concerned with class, but in Southern fiction, and Page's work is representative, it is the determining factor: "The South had been overwhelmed, not whipped, and the indomitable spirit of her people survived" (XIII, 330).

The essays included in *The Old Dominion* that describe the historical and social background out of which the Southern hero emerges look backwards in time; they represent Page's last full attempt to record the manners and customs of his past, to emphasize the "cardinal elements" that "made the Saxon" and the Southerner. Occasionally he reflects upon the Southern past, but in the new century his attention was increasingly drawn to the loss of a certain noble behavior. *Gordon Keith* and *John Marvel,* the two large novels that he wrote in 1903 and 1909, respectively, take the Southern hero away from his provincial background and demonstrate how the code of behavior that he has inherited from generations of Southerners withstands and triumphs over the corruptions of the outside world.

CHAPTER 5

The Vanity of Wealth

I Gordon Keith

A LENGTHY, ambitious novel, *Gordon Keith* (1903) is a disorganized book that illustrates Page's central problem as a writer. In his early stories he provides a suitable setting for his Southern gentleman by evoking a dream-like past in which realism is not demanded—local color becomes a substitute for characterization, even at times for story itself. In *Red Rock* the dream becomes a nightmare—the Southern past is now desecrated, charged with the pathos that attends the fall of a civilization. Page relies not only on local color but on history as well, and there is the sense of his dealing with material that carries its own significance. Throughout the early stories and *Red Rock*, the code of Southern heroism is always implicit and at times banal, but it is rooted to a time and place that Page had deeply felt.

In *Gordon Keith* Page is a local colorist who has forsaken local color; he tries futilely to move along with the mainstream of American literature. He writes his "novel of manners" in an age when the vanity of wealth is a favorite subject of American novelists, but he grounds his theme exclusively on the concept of Southern heroism. "Gordon Keith was the son of a gentleman," he warns us on the first page of the novel. "And this fact, like the cat the honest miller left to his youngest son, was his only patrimony. And in that case also, it stood to the possessor in the place of a good many other things. It helped him over many rough places. He carried it with him as a devoted Romanist wears a sacred scapulary next to the heart" (VI, 1).

In the narrative that follows, Page demonstrates how the code of Southern heroism that Gordon Keith has learned serves him in the modern world. There is no other thematic or narrative or symbolic center to this novel. The chivalric hero, whose roots belong to a nineteenth-century society—his father "knew the Past and lived in it; the Present he did not understand, and the Future he did now know" (VI, 1)—confronts the inequities of city life where money is the vain pursuit of people. Gordon Keith, of course, triumphs morally over the corruption of the city. But the reader does not believe in his triumph or in the author's criticism of the modern world as personified by the city; for, throughout the novel, his hero is attracted to just those characteristics of urban life that he denigrates—to wealth, sophisticated glamor, and class snobbery. Whatever objections Page offers to New York society depend on a literary attitude he has inherited from other sentimental writers; the invidious comparisons he makes between the country and the city strike the reader as automatic responses that are not demonstrated or made credible in the novel itself:

> He [Gordon Keith] began to find himself fitting more and more into the city life. He had the chance possibly to become rich, richer than ever, and with it to secure a charming companion. Why should he not avail himself of it? Amid the glitter and gayety of his surroundings in the city, this temptation grew stronger and stronger. . . . He was becoming "a fair counterfeit" of the men he had once despised. Then came a new form of temptation. What power this wealth would give him! How much good he could accomplish with it!
>
> When the temptation grew too overpowering he left his office and went down into the country. It always did him good to go there. . . . He had been so long in the turmoil and strife of the struggle for success—for wealth; had been so wholly surrounded by those who strove, tearing and trampling and rending those who were in their way, that he had almost lost sight of the life that lay outside of the dust and din of that arena. He had almost forgotten that life held other rewards than riches. He had forgotten the calm and tranquil region that stretched beyond the moil and anguish of the strife for gain.
>
> Here his father walked with him again, calm, serene, and elevated, his thoughts high above all commercial matters, ranging the fields of lofty speculation with statesmen, philosophers, and poets, holding up to his gaze again lofty ideals; practising, without a thought of reward, the very gospel of universal gentleness and kindness.

There his mother, too, moved in spirit once more beside him
with her angelic smile, breathing the purity of heaven. How far
away it seemed from that world in which he had been living!—
as far as they were from the worldlings who made it. (VII, 397,
398, 399)

These attitudes are purely mechanical—in actuality, the city is
attractive. Whatever sylvan retreat the author has in mind is a
figment of his imagination, a childhood memory of bucolic
peace; country life is not described at all in this novel.

Gordon Keith is the son of a gentleman. That is all the reader
needs to know about his character. The statement defines his
heritage and the legacy he brings into the twentieth-century
world. The older Keith—General Keith—is a thin old man; and,
like so many of the fathers of these Southern heroes, he is weary
and shattered, a victim of the Civil War. Gordon Keith rises
from the ravished South, which is only alluded to in the early
sections of the novel but which has the powerful function of
pre-history; from this defeated land, from the lost plantation,
Gordon Keith takes all that remains to him: the code of the
Southern hero. But it is enough—eventually his loyalty to the
code, a higher kind of morality, distinguishes him from the mean,
avaricious Northerners.

Early in the novel, before Page sends his hero away from the
South, he describes a lonely, aristocratic Northern family that
dwells near Gordon Keith and his father. Mrs. Yorke, the mother,
does not believe in the past that General Keith recalls for her,
but the point of view is so biased that it is impossible for the
reader to believe in her disbelief. She rejects Gordon's pursuit
of her daughter Alice because he is impoverished: "she [Alice]
has had the best advantages, and has a right to expect the best
that can be given her . . . an establishment." The author's purpose is made clear as Keith challenges her with the statement:
"You mean money?" She can only answer: "Why, not in the way
in which you put it; but what money stands for—comforts,
luxuries, position" (VI, 184). The point Page wishes to make—
and it is made repeatedly throughout the novel—is that real
aristocracy is measured not by wealth but by blood: the real
aristocrat is finally the person who has a disdain for money.
Any intelligent man, as Gordon Keith proves throughout the
course of the book, can earn money.

Setting the early sections of his novel on a plantation, which clearly represents a Southern paradise—or at least the memory of one—Page leads his protagonist into various circles outside of that moral center; and each circle represents a different form of decay. At first Gordon Keith tries to make his fortune as an engineer in a railroad company located near a small city, Gumbolt, in the Appalachian Mountain range; he meets prostitutes, dancers, those "new" women who pander to the workers and who tempt him into evil.

Gumbolt is a kind of hell that is obvious, and it leads Gordon Keith away from the pristine plantation toward the second kind of hell that dominates the novel—the city. This romantic hero, with his sense of tradition and stability, enters a New York social life that is corrupt at its center, one that is burdened by hypocrisy, greed, and cruelty. Keith meets various representatives of New York society—the Wentworths, the Lancasters, and the Wickershams—each of whom is a moral foil to the hero. The Wentworths divorce each other, largely because of financial difficulties; a Lancaster dies and leaves a widow (formerly Alice Yorke) who is controlled by social snobbery; Frederic Wickersham, once wealthy, declines financially because of spiritual corruption. All of these characters are too obviously contrasted with Gordon Keith—they function too apparently as anti-code heroes.

One of the heroines, Alice Lancaster, illustrates the contrast between Gordon Keith and the other characters most clearly. For Alice, Gordon Keith suggests Romance; her husband—a wealthy New Yorker—represents Reality. The South, Alice believes, is an old-fashioned place where manners are crucial; the North, a modern stronghold in which money determines the fate of people. But for Keith, money is unequivocally an expression of evil: "They [New Yorkers] lived to amass wealth, yet went like sheep in flocks, and were so blind that they could not recognize a great opportunity when it was presented. They were machines that ground through life as monotonously as the wheels in their factories, turning out riches, riches, riches" (VI, 388). Gordon Keith has made money and now he scorns it: money is evanescent, he knows, but ideals are permanent. "He made you live in Arthur's court," Page asserts, "because he lived there himself" (VI, 384).

The previous observations suggest an order and structure that

Gordon Keith does not have. There is no central strand other than Gordon Keith's uncertain movements to hold the narrative together. Besides the obvious fact that Page was incapable of adequately organizing the novel form, he fails here because he does not know his material, or because in a very real sense it horrifies him. Once he has separated himself from the plantation and especially the pre-war South, the smooth flow of manners, marriage, and faithful family life is gone. Gordon Keith, who looks at New York and sees the Wentworths grow estranged and Wickersham connive and steal, is convinced that society has become corrupt because of industrialization. The book is ultimately unreal, a rambling *bildungsroman* about a dislocated boy who finds himself in an alien modern world.

In that alien world Gordon Keith maintains his singular position, uninfluenced by those around him. His father's views on feminism suggest the firmness of that position: "What do you want? One of these sophisticated, fashionable, strong-minded women—a woman's-rights woman? Heaven forbid! When a gentleman marries, he wants a lady and he wants a wife, a woman to love him; a lady to preside over his home, not over a woman's meeting" (VII, 132).

The most impressive quality of *Gordon Keith* is the hero's struggle with New York society life: that struggle results in a nightmare vision of the twentieth century. Page presents Gordon Keith and his father, General Keith, as figures who journey through a dreamlike world in which the well-to-do people and what they earn have no substance: "When General Keith left Brookford he was almost as much in love with his young hostess as his son could have been, and all the rest of his journey he was dreaming of what life might become if Gordon and she would take a fancy to each other, and once more return to the old place. It would be like turning back the years and reversing the consequences of the war . . . I do not know what it is; but there is something in Society that, after a few years, takes away the bloom of ingenuousness and puts in its place just the least little shade of unreality" (VII, 131-179).

Nurtured on plantation life, the Keiths have a solid sense of security that none of the Northerners feels. The Keiths have witnessed plantation life, the Civil War, and the terrors of Reconstruction, and they carry with them the memory of the great Southern civilization before it was debased. Now, leaving the

South for the first time, they are horrified at the outside world.
The movement is more than simply the traditional journey of
the young man from the provinces to the city; it is the nightmare
of the Southern hero who must adapt to other modes of existence. All of the author's fiction leads inevitably to *Gordon Keith;*
and Keith is, without doubt, Page himself. *In Ole Virginia* and
the early stories evoke the Old South and its stability; *Red Rock*
recalls the horror of Reconstruction, but still the old values are
assumed. In *Gordon Keith* he leads his protagonist away from
the South, and the social explosion that occurs is partially caused
by the fact that he has never seen any life other than the
Southern. His seclusion results in a credible conflict between the
nineteenth-century agrarian South and the twentieth-century
industrialized North.

The conclusion of the novel asserts the triumph of the code of
Southern heroism. Gordon Keith has saved his wife Lois Huntington from the malevolence of Wickersham; he has befriended
and sustained a dancing girl, Terpsichore (modeled, incidentally,
after Bret Harte's "noble women of easy virtue"); he has re-
trieved Lady Wentworth's money, stolen by the bankrupt
Wickersham; he has rescued Norman Wentworth from financial
trouble. The various failures and inadequacies of those Northerners whom Keith aids are due to the absence of any code of
values similar to the hero's. Indeed, Gordon Keith himself fears
that he will adopt the promiscuous, undisciplined lives of his
new associates:

> Keith sat and reflected. How different he was from his father!
> How different from what he had been years ago! Then he had
> had an affection for the old home and all that it represented. He
> had worked with the idea of winning it back some day. It had
> been an inspiration to him. But now it was wealth that he had
> begun to seek.
>
> It came to him clearly how much he had changed. The process
> all lay before him. It had grown with his success, and had kept
> pace with it in an almost steady ratio since he had set success
> before him as a goal. He was angry with himself to find that he
> was thinking now of success merely as Wealth. Once he had
> thought of Honor and Achievement, even of Duty. He remem-
> bered when he had not hesitated to descend into what appeared
> the very jaws of death, because it seemed to him his duty. He
> wondered if he would do the same now. (VII, 330-31)

Keith returns to his well-established, traditional behavior but only through great self-discipline. He helps to restore order to lives that have been broken by divorce, embezzlement, adultery, and prostitution—corruptions that are an outgrowth of modern urban living. Keith marries Lois Huntington, whom he has pursued for some time, and when his father comes to New York to live with the young couple, his patriarchal views are welcomed by the young couple. After a rather tortured journey through the iniquitous city, Gordon Keith emerges scarred but essentially healthy; indeed, he has converted Northerners to the belief that the code of Southern heroism is the most serviceable guide to life in the twentieth century. General Keith, the father, remains, more a spirit than a person; his presence constantly reminds the younger Keiths of the solid tradition that lies behind them.

Contemporary criticism recognized the obvious limitations of the book, characterizing it as "prolix" and structurally weak and chastising Page for emphasizing hereditary values, for changing his setting from the South to the North.[1] One of the most interesting and perceptive reviews—actually a review of the entire Plantation edition, published four years later in 1907—noted the change in Page, the differences between *Red Rock* and *Gordon Keith;* the article, symptomatically entitled "The Waning Influence of Thomas Nelson Page," went on to emphasize the inadequacy of his code of heroism for the twentieth-century reader:

Now, something has happened in the South during the last ten years so radical and so overwhelming that what was true is now history, what was characteristic has become bombastic, and what were principles of living are mere sentimentalities, connected with the *code duello* existence of the past. Whether this is due to the fact that a younger, less prejudiced generation has reached up, taken the book from Mr. Page's hand, read it, tested it, and laid it down with strange indifference, or whether commercialism has rendered us too sordid to appreciate the ideality for which his writings stand, it is impossible to say. But the fact remains that the South has outgrown Mr. Page one way or the other. The spirit of the South dramatized in his books is no longer sufficiently related to this new spirit to command its interest and obeisance. This accounts in a great measure for the comparative failure of 'Gordon Keith,' after the immense popularity of 'Red Rock.' The scenes of both stories cover practically the same period of reconstruction, both are based upon the same ideals of unimpeachable honor, of courage in adversity, and of being gentle according to the length of one's pedigree. But it happens that "Gordon Keith" was published five years later, when even Mr. Page's readers had grown weary of the eternal psalm about ante-bellum greatness and post-bellum martyrs. This is not an evidence of decadence but of returning strength. Thus, in the South they suddenly realized that Gordon Keith was a post-humous knight, the italics of a type of manhood no longer convenient to imitate. They had become suddenly interested in something else, in the future, that challenging, immeasurable future upon the walls of which no grandfather's swords hang to claim it. Henceforth the novelist of Southern life must change his scene, bring it forward. And Mr. Page can no more do this than he can change his name and his genius. Both belong essentially to the past, and as a part of it they command respect, admiration, even reverence, but no longer absorbing interest.[2]

Gordon Keith is an attempt to write a novel of society similar to that of James and Howells; but Page does not know the segment he writes of, and he has no clear understanding of the motivations that drive his characters to seek wealth. Unable to create human beings, he creates types; unable to give the conflict and situations a sense of verisimilitude, he presents tableaux of deterioration, involving bankruptcy, divorce, peculation, prostitution, and feminism. But these scenes are unimpressive because they are not rooted in the behavior of human beings; they are stock situations which too obviously are meant to dramatize the spiritual decay caused by industrialization. Money, the central subject of this novel, is the symbol of evil. The contrasts between Gordon Keith and the wealthy New Yorkers, between the barren South and the munificent North, and between the ravished country and the corrupt city are all too facile and mechanical. It is all too clear that the hero himself is fascinated by money, that his success in the world of finance gives him great self-esteem, and that his platitudes on the evil consequences of money are hollow beside his obvious attraction to it.

II Under the Crust

Occasionally, in this "waning" period of his career, Page wrote children's stories, such as "Santa Claus's Partner" (1899) and "Tommy Trot's Visit to Santa Claus" (1908); these tales for young people are full of sentimental, safe adventures and happy endings. The influence of Dickens, and especially of "The Christmas Carol," is most evident in the former story in which an irascible millionaire named Livingstone is incapable of enjoying Christmas: "Success had come to mean but one thing for him: Gold: he no longer strove for honor but for riches" (VIII, 210). But the old man is converted to charity and benevolence by one of the many children of his employee—he becomes "Santa Claus's Partner" and bestows gifts upon the poor. This same theme—the vanity of wealth, the superiority of the heart to the head—can be found in most of the stories that Page wrote at the turn of the century.

These tales, like *Gordon Keith* and *John Marvel, Assistant,* use threadbare motives and draw predictable morals. The comparison of the peaceful past with the crude present, the inevitable corruption that money brings, the lack of responsibility on the part of the younger generation—these themes appear throughout his fiction. One should note, however, that the themes, as genuine as they may seem in each particular case, are mere literary gestures, completely at odds with Page's political and social views. "The fact that by 1900 he had embraced one of the extreme implications of the term ["the New South"], a desire to see the South industrialized by Northern capital, did not minimize his determination to see the old South memorialized and vindicated";[3] and his private life in the early 1900's was more similar to that of his wealthy characters before their conversion to the life of the spirit—like Berryman Livingstone in "Santa Claus's Partner," Page "was a man of taste and culture, a gentleman of refinement. He spent his money like a gentleman, to surround himself with objects of art and to give himself and his friends pleasure" (VIII, 178). Yet he churned out stories that automatically criticized the twentieth-century addiction to wealth and industrialization. The title given to the volume of stories in the Plantation Edition suggests the general intention: *Under the Crust* implies that beneath the surface of superficial manners there is little heroic substance in modern man; there has been, he laments in a typical article of this period, a general "decay of manners."[4]

"Miss Godwin's Inheritance" (1904) is a local-color story that attempts to capture the flavor of Maine—it is more a state of emotion than a narrative or a story. A local farmer, Silas Free-

man—whose name suggests his freedom from urbanized convention—extols the virtues of the country as opposed to the stifling
atmosphere of the city. Silas forms a friendship with the narrator's cousin, Hortensia, who has moved to her grandfather's summer home in Maine because she has an appreciation for the
country and the past that her grandfather represents to her. So
attached is she to the past, in fact, that she intends to restore the
place as her grandfather knew it years before—and Miss Godwin,
who was once a lover of Hortensia's grandfather, is to help her.

The decay of moral standards that results from avarice now
dominates Page's fiction. In "The New Agent at Lebanon Station" (1905), a young innocent hero dupes a covetous villain
into returning property to its lawful owner; in "A Brother to
Diogenes," the narrator, an avaricious investor in the stock
market, takes a vacation and meets an old man—Page's American
version of the Ancient Mariner—who has traveled the world for
wealth but who has discovered that a man ought to enjoy life
and not worry about acquiring a fortune. In "A Goth" (1907),
an older man, an incorrigible gambler, refuses to take the money
he has won from a young boy called Newman because the boy
has been using his father's fortune—Page denigrates those young
men who travel through Europe irresponsibly, living a dandified
life at the expense of their fathers.[5] In "Leander's Light" (1907),
an old man refuses to sell his summer home to an opportunist—
instead, he leaves it to the town for a hospital or a school, and
so rejects the vulgar materialism of the new generation.[6]

More elaborate than any of these stories attacking materialism
is a story he wrote in 1907 entitled "My Friend, the Doctor."
This tale anticipates the novel *John Marvel, Assistant* that he
was soon to write, and the leading figure, Dr. John Graemen,
resembles that later secular saint, John Marvel. Like John Marvel,
the doctor was a brilliant but casual student in college who
aided the poor—in this case by attending diphtheria cases. Whereas other medical students advanced normally, pursuing their personal careers, the doctor was more interested in people, and he
scorned the fashions and fortunes so important to his colleagues.
He settles in New England and meets his antagonist, Mme.
Durer, who represents the emancipated modern woman: forth-
right and hard, as her name suggests, she is wealthy, pretentious,
and sophisticated.

Mme. Durer comes to the doctor's more natural surroundings

from the city, and she brings her daughter with her. She exhibits little love for the girl ("the womanliness—the motherhood—is all squeezed out of these modern women," the doctor complains), although she rears her child carefully—she is highly indignant, for example, when she discovers that the governess has permitted her child to play with a poor friend. Retribution is inevitable, of course, and it arrives when Mme. Durer's daughter falls ill and dies. Dr. Graemen, who has attended the girl, tells the repentant mother that her child has died of starvation—"in the heart." The story is patently sentimental and melodramatic; Mme. Durer finally confesses that she did not have "a soul in the worl' as cared for her—just cared for the money she had"—and Page underscores the various objects of his attack: inhuman accumulation of wealth, feminism, and pretense. These are the evils that accompany the growing industrialization of the modern world.[7]

One feels a curious contradiction throughout his later fiction which becomes most obvious in *John Marvel, Assistant*: intellectually, Page recognizes the need for an egalitarian society in the twentieth century and he recommends increased industrialization as the solution to the problems of the Negro; however, he is committed to a racist view that is retrogressive. In *Gordon Keith* and the later stories, the contradiction is not so apparent since the moral adversaries emerge from the same nineteenth-century world; but in *John Marvel, Assistant*, Page's last novel, the clash between a nineteenth-century agrarian view and a twentieth-century socialist attitude, between the vestigial aristocracy and the insurgent working class is most apparent—and disastrous. The book indicates how incompatible artistically the life of the industrialized city was to Page.

III   John Marvel, Assistant: *The Vanity of Wealth*

In *John Marvel*, Page describes the world in which he lives rather than a remembered world. He continues to explore the themes that he had developed in *Gordon Keith*, but now he writes with even more directness. Aware of the literary and historical temper of his time, he presents poverty-stricken masses, unemployed workers, striking unionists, idealistic preachers; he creates, like so many of his contemporaries, a novel whose central subject is Christian Socialism and whose pervasive theme is the vanity of wealth. This theme is powerful when treated by Howells, Dreiser, Harold Frederic, or Tourgée (in *Murvale Eastman*); but Page does not know the intricate problems of urban life, and all of his social workers are stereotypes. His underprivileged slum dwellers for example, are imitations of more impressive characters in the realistic fiction of the period. This subject is not suited to his talent, and the reader recoils from the factitious and sentimental narrative of his book.

The point of view suggests his limitations. Henry Glave is the hero of all of his works: the parochial gentleman who witnesses corruption but never shares it, who reports the eccentricities of others and acts as the moral voice of the author. Page develops this character in the first part of his novel so the reader will be able to measure the validity of Henry Glave's later commentary on the manners and mores of his time. He wants Glave to stand for the typical young professional man, an honest and honorable man whose sins are all venial. Glave has a keen sense of family tradition and admits his own inadequacy in carrying on that tradition: "My family was an old and distinguished one; that is, it could be traced back about two hundred years, and several of my ancestors had accomplished enough to be known in the history of the State—a fact of which I was so proud that I was quite satisfied at college to rest on their achievements, and felt no need to add to its distinction by any labors of my own" (XV, 4).

Page is being semi-autobiographical here, for as Henry Glave tells us, his "childhood was spent on an old plantation, so far removed from anything that I have since known that it might almost have been in another planet" (XIV, 4). His rural background gives him the proper innocence against which to measure his experiences; once again, Page writes a novel similar in format to those that take the young boy from the innocence of country life to the inequities of the city.

Glave's education begins in college, a small place that is apparently located in the South. Here he meets the two most significant characters in the novel: Leopold Wolffert and John Marvel. In a chapter entitled "The Jew and the Christian," Page creates an interesting portrait that reveals more about the prejudice and limited perception of the college boys than it does about the Jew:

The fact that a Jew [Leopold Wolffert] had come and taken one of the old apartments spread through the college with amazing rapidity and created a sensation. Not that there had not been Jews there before, for there had been a number there at one time or another. But they were members of families of distinction, who had been known for generations as bearing their part in all the appointments of life, and had consorted with other folk on an absolute equality; so that there was little or nothing to distinguish them as Israelites except their name. If they were Israelites, it was an accident and played no larger part in their views than if they had been Scotch or French. But here was a man who proclaimed himself a Jew; who proposed that it should be known, and evidently meant to assert his rights and peculiarities on all occasions. The result was that he was subjected to a species of persecution which only the young Anglo-Saxon, the most brutal of all animals, could have devised.[8]

These boys are not interested in Wolffert's religion—they, and all of Page's characters, are not really interested in their own religion, whatever formal statement the author may make. Wolffert's genealogy is of paramount importance, and the assumption is that a gentleman will automatically obey the forms of religion. But even in this novel, whose subject is the practical application of Christianity and whose center is so often the church itself, the theological overtones are kept to a minimum. In *John Marvel,* theology surrenders to the message of Christ.

The author's attempt to portray a pugnacious, brilliant uncompromising Jew surrounded by a rigid and parochial community is effective and sometimes moving. The Jew is properly isolated from the Anglo-Saxon culture around him, and this isolation induces in him an attitude of aggression toward, as well as compassion for, the underprivileged. Page struggles too much for fairness, and one can feel his attempt to suppress his own instinctual sense of superiority to Wolffert. But the attitude he ascribes to his white Anglo-Saxon heroine—who represents the highest kind of standard in his moral universe—is really his own:

Her [Eleanor Leigh's] idea of the Israelites had always been curiously connoted with hooked noses, foreign speech of a far from refined type, and a persistent pursuit of shekels by ways generally devious and largely devoted to shops containing articles more or less discarded by other people. Here she found a cultivated gentleman with features, if not wholly classical, at least more regular and refined than those of most young men of her acquaintance; speech so cultivated as to be quite distinguished, and an air and manner so easy and gracious as to suggest her complete knowledge of the great world. No matter what subject was discussed between them, he knew about it more than any one else, and always threw light on it which gave a new interest for her. He had a knowledge of the literature and art, not only of the ancients, but of most modern nations, and he talked to her of things of which she had never so much as heard. He had not only travelled extensively in Europe, but had travelled in a way to give him an intimate knowledge not merely of the countries, but of the people and customs of the countries which no one she had ever met possessed. He had crossed in the steerage of ocean-liners more than once and had stoked across both to England and the Mediterranean. (XV, 160-61)

This modern Ahasuerus wanders through the novel, appearing in the finest sections as an incorrigible defender of humanity who decries the society in which he lives as one which has abandoned the common man. "There was never so selfish and hypocritical a society on earth," he exclaims, "as this which now exists. In times past, under the feudal system, there was apparently some reason for the existence of the so-called upper classes—the first castle built made necessary all the others—the chief, at least, protected the subjects from the rapine of others, and he was always ready to imperil his life; but now—this! When they all claim to know, and do know much, they sit quiet in their own smug content like fatted swine, and let rapine, debauchery, and murder go on as it never has gone on in the last three hundred years" (XVI, 33).

Wolffert leads the factory workers when they strike, thus exposing himself to constant danger. Page is remarkably direct and unsentimental in his presentation of this Jew who refuses to "worship a ritual, or a church" but "only God" (XVI, 206). When Wolffert falls ill, Page vividly describes the base conditions under which he has chosen to live. "I [Henry Glave] found Wolffert sitting up in a chair, but looking wretchedly ill. He, however, declared himself much better. I learned afterward— though not from him—that he had caught some disease while investigating some wretched kennels known as 'lodging houses,' where colonies of Jews were packed like herrings in a barrel;

and for which a larger percentage on the value was charged as rental than for the best dwellings in the city" (XVI, 291). Through Leopold Wolffert, Page reiterates his dominant theme: "What does the worker now know of ideals? He is reduced to a machine, and a very poor machine at that. He does not know where his work goes, or have an interest in it. Give him that. Give his fellows that. It will uplift him, uplift his class, create a great reservoir from which to draw a better class" (XV, 308-9).

Wolffert is killed in a strike, heroic in his extreme behavior, a martyr to the socialism he has championed throughout his life; and his views are those that the author wants the reader to feel most deeply. In depicting the other Jews in *John Marvel, Assistant,* Page retreats to stereotypes that are vulgar; it is curious indeed that Jewish readers of the novel were so content with his views.[9] One suspects, as he reads the dialogue of these minor characters, that Page has no real conception at all of Jewish life and is merely trying to create eccentrics to provide a colorful and at times a bleak background to his major situation. When the narrator visits Wolffert, for example, he sees him living in a Jewish neighborhood that is decadent and corrupt:

> For blocks they filled the sidewalk, moving slowly on, and as I mingled in the mass, and caught low, guttural, unknown sounds, and not a word of English all the while, I became suddenly aware of a strange alien feeling of uncertainty and almost of oppression. Far as eye could see I could not descry one Saxon countenance or even one Teuton. They were all dark, sallow, dingy, and sombre. Now and then a woman's hat appeared in the level moving surge of round black hats, giving the impression of a bubble floating on a deep, slow current to melt into the flood. Could this, I reflected sombrely, be the element we are importing? and what effect would the strange confluence have on the current of our life in the future? No wonder we were in the throes of a strike vast enough to cause anxiety! (XVI, 287)

Leopold Wolffert represents one dimension of Christian Socialism; he is an intemperate, outspoken radical who brings to human affairs the wisdom and the fury, the historicity and confidence of the Old Testament—of Judaism. The titular hero, however, exhibits all those characteristics one associates with Christ: humility, meekness, compassion. Living in the late nineteenth century, John Marvel is clearly an idealization, a minister whose name suits his character. Page never examines him closely, for he is more a symbol than a person; ultimately, he stands for what the people in the novel ought to be and are not.

John Marvel's relationship with the narrator, Henry Glave, is that of the ideal to the real, the perfect to the vulnerable. They grow to know one another in college—even as a collegian Marvel is a poet and an idealist who leaves the college for weeks to conduct a Sunday school in the nearby mountains. He is at the bottom of his class, but in Page's moral universe that is creditable: gentlemen can always do well in school; gentlemen can always make money. Marvel is a shadowy figure in the novel. He rarely speaks, for Page does not wish to destroy his ideality by making him too real a character; and when periodically he does appear, he silently acts out the role of saint: he works with the poor, he aids diphtheria victims in a mining camp, and he helps strikers achieve better working conditions. Marvel's thematic function is to remind the various characters of their moral reality.

Eleanor Leigh, the heroine of the novel, is the daughter of a wealthy factory owner, socially well placed and unconcerned with the problems of the poor. At first, she feels aloof to John Marvel because of his physical awkwardness and his lack of poise; but she learns that he is kind, and shortly she is assisting him with the poor. For the first time in her life she feels useful; and, as the author describes her, she becomes a woman reborn: "As Eleanor Leigh stepped out into the morning light, she looked on a new earth, as fair as if it had just been created, and it was a new Eleanor Leigh who gazed upon it. The tinsel of frivolity had shrivelled and perished in the fire of that night. Sham had laid bare its shallow face and fled away. Life had taken on reality. She had seen a man, and thenceforth only a man could command her" (XV, 173).

Henry Glave, the protagonist of the novel, is also spiritually guided by John Marvel. Glave's development provides the narrative center of the book. After struggling to receive a law degree, falling in and out of love with a heartless woman, and failing in politics, this prodigal son invests money in the stock market and soon is bankrupt. But, like the typical Page hero, he has fallen only to rise again, fallen so that he can become more dramatically committed to the moral life: "a new man took my place within me," he observes, as he is rejected by his lady, and "I was passed into a man of resolution" (XV, 67).

Glave wanders westward in search of his fortune and discovers that avarice and selfishness are the chief traits of those people he meets: a successful cousin refuses him employment, a newspaperman cares only for sensational gossip, a well-dressed minister panders to wealthy members of his congregation. In sundry similar ways, Page introduces the central theme of the novel:

> The vulgar make the parade; the refined pass so quietly as scarcely to be observed. The vulgarity of the display of riches began to oppress me. I discovered later the great store of refinement, goodness, and sweetness that was hidden in the homes alike of an element of the wealthy, the merely well-to-do, and the poor. But for a time it was all eclipsed by the glare of the vulgar and irresponsible rich. Arrogance, discontent, hardness, vulgarity, were stamped in many faces, and spoke in every movement of many of those I saw, even of the most richly dressed. . . . They [the wealthy] have no traditions and no ideals. They know no standard but wealth, and possess no ability to display it but through parade. . . . They think that wealth has exempted them from decency. They mistake civility for servility and rudeness for gentility. Their best effort is only a counterfeit, a poor imitation of what they imagine to be the manners of the upper class abroad whose indifferent manners they ape. (XV, 244-45)

This statement about the vanity of wealth is gratuitous and poorly placed in the novel since by this time the hero has failed in his attempt to realize his material ambitions, and his moralizing is specious and offensive. Furthermore Henry Glave is not prepared to live modestly—he turns to gambling and even thinks of committing suicide when he sees no way out of his financial difficulties. Most of his statements about the vanity of wealth are theoretical at best—in each specific incident that concerns the poverty-stricken, he responds like a man wearing white gloves in the slums. Hearing the story of a prostitute, for example, he cringes in horror. The girl has been forced into prostitution by a man, and the narrator's reaction is significant. "The man who had secured her heart," Page writes, "used his power over her to seize and sell her into a slavery for which there is no name which could be used on the printed page. Here, stricken by the horror of her situation, she had attempted to escape from her captors, but had been bodily beaten into submission. Then she had made a wild dash for liberty and had been seized and slashed with a knife until she fell under the wounds and her life was in imminent danger" (XV, 260).

This Dostoevskian situation—one is reminded of the last scene in *Notes from Underground*—has no ironic overtones in Page's hands. Henry Glave is very simply horrified at the prostitute, and he shrinks from her. Page, because of the very nature of his material, has sent his major figure into a situation that demands realistic treatment, that insists upon a human response; but he recoils from slums and prostitutes and keeps his character fundamentally a caricature—now disastrously a caricature of the Southern hero. Glave's inability to respond humanly to the incidents and people he witnesses is Page's unintended admission that the code of heroism which served so well for his antebellum Southern heroes is not suited to a changing world. Page is too honest not to realize that the society he now lives in is unstable, but his protagonist is like an amnesia victim suddenly thrust into the modern world. He does not know how to behave.

This world—which dominates the second volume of the novel— is one that involves the social problems of factory workers. The author creates a typical strike scene in which the laborers, led by an unattractive leader called Wringman, demand 15 percent more money; Mr. Leigh, the employer and father of the heroine, is firm in his resistance to the strikers. Leigh's position in the novel reflects Page's difficulty, for traditionally—as father of the heroine and a gentleman—Leigh would be sympathetically drawn; but here he is the capitalist leader and the opponent of the working class and of the moral spokesmen of the novel, John Marvel and Leopold Wolffert. Page's solution is to project Leigh as an employer who is very sympathetic to the workers but who, in his financially depressed position, is overcome by their avaricious attitudes. These workers, as a minor character points out, are interested only in money: "Ze music iss dead—ze harmony iss all gone—in ze people—in ze heart! Zere iss no more music in ze souls of ze people. It iss monee—monee—monee—fight, fight, fight all ze time! Who can gife ze divine strain ven ze heart is set on monee always?" And then the narrator reflects: "Who indeed? I thought, and the more I thought of it the more clearly I felt that he had touched the central truth" (XVI, 116-17).

Page transfers the unattractive qualities that readers might normally associate with Leigh to a supporter of his, Reverend Capon, whose assistant and obvious moral foil is John Marvel. Capon supports only wealthy churchgoers who of course support him; and when Marvel permits Wolffert to speak in his church, thus arousing the indignation of a wealthy parishioner, Capon strongly censures his assistant and Marvel resigns. Even here Page blurs the moral force of his novel when his narrator begins to speak like an equivocating politician: "I do not mean in relating Dr. Capon's position in this interview to make any charge against others who might honestly hold the same view which he held as to the propriety of John Marvel's having requested Leo Wolffert to speak in his church, however I myself might differ from the point of view . . ." (XV, 203). Such flatulent observations obscure the point of view and dull what might otherwise have been—as *The Damnation of Theron Ware* and *Murvale Eastman* are—a sharp attack on the secular church.

The basic reason that *John Marvel, Assistant* fails is that Page has selected material that properly belongs to a "problem novel" and finds himself, in the process of writing it, unwilling or perhaps unable to explore and understand the world he has entered. His whole tradition—literary as well as social—argues against this kind of material; for now money matters, the underprivileged insist on asserting their rights, and social conditions change so quickly that the heroes of a pre-war period easily become the villains, or at least the antagonists, of the twentieth-century world. The narrator, who clearly speaks for the author, tells his future wife, Eleanor Leigh, how opposed he is to the problem novel, to precisely that kind of novel he is narrating: "it is all in the manner—the motive. I have no objection to the matter [of the modern novel]—generally, provided it be properly handled—but the obvious intention—the rank indecentness of it. See how Scott or George Eliot or Tolstoi or Turgenieff or, later on, even Zola, handles such vital themes. How different their motive from the reeking putrescence of the so-called problem novel" (XVI, 246).

The last portion of *John Marvel, Assistant* functions on two levels: the traditional one in which Henry Glave pursues Eleanor Leigh and eventually marries her, and the more contemporary one which describes the death and martyrdom of Wolffert and the saintliness of John Marvel. The second level is the more impressive because it is the more truthful. Wolffert, living in his ghetto, is by far the most dramatic and credible character in the novel—the real hero, as Rosewell Page realized.[10] And when Wolffert cries out for the dignity of the working man, he elicits all of Page's sympathy and admiration: "What does the worker now know of ideals? He is reduced to a machine, and a very poor machine at that. He does not know where his work goes, or have an interest in it. Give him that. Give his fellows that. It will uplift him, uplift his class, create a great reservoir from which to draw a better class" (XV, 308-9). When this man is killed in the strike, the moral of the book is drawn:

> I never fully knew until after his death how truly Wolffert was one of the Prophets. I often think of him with his high aim to better the whole human race, inspired by a passion for his own people to extend his ministration to all mankind, cast out by those he labored for; denying that he was a Christian, and yet dying a Christian death in the act of supplicating for those who slew him. I owe him a great debt for teaching me many things, but chiefly for the knowledge that the future of the race rests on the whole people and its process depends on each one, however he may love his own, working to the death for all. He opened my eyes to the fact that every man who contributes to the common good of mankind is one of the chosen people and that the fundamental law is to do good to mankind." (XVI, 329-30)

Glave, who reports this, does not live according to what he learns; and Page, by having his narrator marry Eleanor Leigh, returns comfortably to the sentimental situation present in his other fiction. Wolffert is dead and does not disturb the peace of these two stock characters; the strike, the riot, the problems of working-class people—all that has engaged the narrator's attention in his moral development—now vanish as if they had never existed. Glave certainly remains unchanged. His last remarks appear particularly unctuous and unconvincing, poor platitudes that the typical hero of the sentimental novel addresses to the reader: "She slipped her hand in my arm, and a warm feeling for all mankind surged about my heart" (XVI, 356).

John Marvel, Assistant is an imbalanced novel in which Page tries unsuccessfully to merge old forms with new, the materials of traditional sentiment with socialistic concerns that demand a complete commitment on the part of the writer. It is hard to conceive of a novelist less suited to a sympathetic description of socialism than Page: all of his inclinations are opposed to egalitarianism, and whatever tribute he pays to the underprivileged emerges as artificial and even condescending. This novel, published in 1909, was a futile attempt to write the kind of novel that was being written more successfully by Dreiser and Norris and Howells: there is an "absence of nearly everything which" the reader has come to regard as characteristic of Page.[11] In trying to cater to the changing tastes of his audience, he merely indicated that his best subject was the distant past before the Civil War when he did not have to contend with a changing, unstable society.

Even so sympathetic a critic as Arthur Hobson Quinn, who completely accepted Page's version of the ante-bellum South and Reconstruction, is forced to conclude that

> "In his novels Mr. Page is working on a larger canvas, and the canvas seems at times to be a looser texture. The finish of style, the charm of diction which characterize the short stories are not so marked in the longer books; and by reason of their very nature, unity of tone cannot be secured so well. There is a hint of the melodramatic, too, in *Gordon Keith* and in *John Marvel, Assistant*. Things happen *too* conveniently, and the way in which the hero of the latter book recalls conversations of which he could have had no knowledge almost takes one's breath away. . . . There are many who can paint the railroad strikes of *John Marvel* or the speculation of *Gordon Keith;* no one but a Southern gentleman could have written *Red Rock* or *Meh Lady*."[12]

IV   *Robert E. Lee*

The hero of the fixed, agrarian society and the great historical figure who serves as the prototype of the Southern gentleman is Robert E. Lee. Page's admiration for Lee is boundless, and the book that he published in 1909 as *Robert E. Lee: The Southerner* and then in a vastly improved form as *Robert E. Lee: Man and Soldier* [1911] is more hagiography than biography. Page confesses at the outset that his work is written "in obedience to a feeling that as the son of a Confederate soldier, as a Southerner, as an American, he, as a writer, owes something to himself and his countrymen"—and he writes the book with a sense of great dedication. "The subject," he warns himself and his readers, "is not to be dealt with in the language of eulogy. To attempt to decorate it with panegyric would but belittle it" (XVII, xvii). For the most part, in tracing Lee's career as a soldier, Page is quite restrained; but when he describes Lee's character, he eulogizes the man as though he is writing from an inflexible and automatic literary point of view—what was human becomes symbolic; what was individual surrenders to stereotype.

The relationship between the author and the general sets the tone of the book. Page remembers himself as one of many young men who thought of Lee as a spiritual father. He attended Washington-Lee College when Lee was president; his own father was also one of Lee's "old soldiers" who, "often at great sacrifice, sent their sons to be under his direction, and to learn at his feet the stern lesson of duty" (XVIII, 342). Page feels a personal obligation to Lee. "It was high privilege," he recalls, "to know him when I was a boy. It was also my privilege to see something of that army which followed him throughout the war, and on whose courage and fortitude his imperishable glory as a captain is founded. I question whether in all the army under his command was one man who had his genius; but I believe that in character he was but the type of his order, and as noble as was his, ten thousand gentlemen marched behind him who, in all the elements of private character, were his peers" (XVIII, 375).

With these attitudes Page approaches his subject. He traces the ancestry of Lee, which dates from 1641 and which had been continually Virginian through the seventeenth, eighteenth, and nineteenth centuries. Lee himself was born on January 19, 1807; in his childhood, he modelled himself after that other Virginian, George Washington—"as Washington was the consummate flower of the life of Colonial Virginia," Page observes, "so Lee, clinging close to 'his precious example' became the perfect fruit of her later civilization" (XVIII, 375). In the first part of his biography, Page concentrates on Lee's attitude toward slavery and the Civil War, indicating that Lee supported emancipation of the slaves and in fact set free his own slaves before the war. Like Page's own father, Lee did not want to fight in the war; and one of the most moving sections is the description of Lee's tortured decision to support the South as opposed to the Union whose armies he had served. "The President of the United States [had] tendered to him the command of the armies of the Union about to take the field. . . . But Lee had from his boyhood been reared in the Southern school of States' Rights as interpreted by the conservative statesmen of Virginia" (XVII, 47, 54). By quoting from the various letters that Lee wrote to his military superiors, relatives, and friends, Page makes the general's agonizing choice dramatically real for the reader:

> With all my devotion to the Union [Lee wrote to his sister, whose husband espoused the Union Cause], and the feeling of loyalty and duty of an American citizen, I have not been able to make up my mind to raise my hand against my relatives, my children, my home. I have, therefore, resigned my commission in the army, and save in defence of my native State, with the sincere hope that my poor services may never be needed, I hope I may never be called on to draw my sword. I know you will blame me; but you must think as kindly of me as you can, and believe that I have endeavored to do what I thought right. (XVII, 76-77).

Once Virginia was involved in the war, however, Lee had no choice, and by June 1, 1862, he had assumed command of the Confederate forces. Page records the battles with verve and excitement, and one follows Lee's adventures at Richmond, Antietam, Fredericksburg, and Gettysburg. He also balances Lee's public career with his private life, and in numerous letters to his wife, the general emerges as a simple, pious, and considerate man. He also emerges as the great general that he was—offensively as well as defensively—a leader who brought dignity to the Southern cause.

In defeat, Lee maintains that dignity; he still commands the "devotion of the South." Lee becomes, in the later portions of this long, affectionate biography, the historical counterpart to General Keith and John Marvel; upon retiring from the army he is offered many remunerative positions, and he refuses them:

> On one of these occasions he was approached with a tender of the presidency of an insurance company at a salary of $50,000 a year. He declined it on the ground that it was work with which he was not familiar. "But, general," said the gentleman who represented the insurance company, "you will not be expected to do any work; what we wish is the use of your name."
> "Do you not think," said General Lee, "that if my name is worth $50,000 a year, I ought to be very careful about taking care of it?"

Amid the commercialism of the present age this sounds as refreshing as the oath of a knight of the Round Table. (XVIII, 326)

The reader has really come full circle in Page's career. His biography of Lee, in spite of its great and accurate concentration on individual battles, is like the epitome of all his fiction: the early life of Lee is similar to the early experiences of the heroes in "Marse Chan" and "On Newfound River"; the heroism in battle is that of Southern gentlemen (although usually assumed in the fiction); the noble and physically weak Lee of the post-bellum period is Dr. Cary of *Red Rock*, General Keith of *Gordon Keith*, and the fathers of innumerable other heroes and heroines in the short stories; the pious Lee who withstands the tempting offers of the commercial world is Gordon Keith and John Marvel, and the heroes of Page's last work of fiction, *The Land of the Spirit* (1913). The summation of Lee's character suggests how the general represents to the writer the highest qualities of the Southern gentleman:

History may be searched in vain to find Lee's superior, and only once or twice in its long course will be found his equal. To find his prototype, we must go back to ancient times, to the antique heroes who have been handed down to us by Plutarch's matchless portraiture; yet, as we read their story, we see that we have been given but one side of their character. Their weaknesses have mainly been lost in the lapse of centuries, and their virtues are magnified in the enhaloing atmosphere of time. But, as to Lee, we know his every act.

There was no act or incident of his life on which a light as fierce as that which beats upon a throne did not fall. He was investigated by high commissions; his every act was examined by hostile prosecutors. His conduct was inquired into by those who had every incentive of hostility to secure his downfall and his degradation. Yet, amid these fierce assaults, he remained as unmoved as he had stood when he had held the heights of Fredericksburg against the furious attacks of Burnside's intrepid infantry. From this inquisition he came forth as unspoiled as the mystic White Knight of the Round Table. In that vivid glare he stood revealed in the full measure of nobility—the closest scrutiny but brought forth new virtues and disclosed a more rounded character:

"Like Launcelot brave, like Galahad clean." (XVIII, 371-72)

This description, as burdened as it is by eulogistic rhetoric, is fundamentally true—more dispassionate accounts of Lee vindicate Page's general estimate. But Page needs to raise his eyes away from Lee for only a moment to give all Southern soldiers the same noble traits as their leader; thus he blurs the picture, making it more fictional than historical:

> As I have immersed myself in the subject of this great captain and noble gentleman, there has appeared to troop before me from a misty past that army on whose imperishable deeds, inspired by love of liberty, is founded the fame of possibly the greatest soldier of our race—that army of the South, composed not only of the best that the South had, but wellnigh of all she had. Gentle and simple, old and young, rich and poor, secessionist and anti-secessionist, with every difference laid aside at the call of duty, animated by one common spirit, love of liberty, they flocked to the defence of the Southern States. Through four years they withstood to the utmost the fiercest assaults of fortune, and submitted only with their annihilation. . . .
> . . . Of them, in conclusion, we may use the words of Pericles, spoken over the Athenian dead who fell in the Peloponnesian War:
> "So died these men as became Athenians. . . ." (XVIII, 375-76)

All those characteristics attributed to the Southern hero—truth, honor, loyalty, military discipline, an inflexible social posture, manners, courtesy, hospitality, sectional chauvinism—find their greatest fruition in Robert E. Lee. For Page, Lee is the finest incarnation of the Southern hero; and there is no greater praise in Page's moral lexicon.

V The Land of the Spirit

The fact that Page wrote his biography of Lee at the same time as *John Marvel, Assistant* led him into pointed commentaries on the hero's refusal, after the war, to capitulate to the new commercialism of American society. Shortly after the publication of *John Marvel* and *Robert E. Lee,* he wrote several stories in which the vanity of wealth once again becomes the dominant theme. The title of this collection of tales, *The Land of the Spirit* (1913), suggests Page's concerns: "Duty to God and duty to our neighbor," he states in the preface, "have come almost suddenly to assume a new and personal meaning" in the modern world. "Out of this fresh moral consciousness have grown most of the new moral movements in our day, and much the larger part of the spiritual forces that have had their birth in our time. From taking thought only of the things of the body we have come to ponder the treasures of the soul, and the new light has shown us that the field is no longer confined to a future state in some distant heaven, but lies here actually in our midst."[13]

The stories illustrate his concern with Christian Socialism. "The Stranger's Pew" tells of a preacher who has served the poor, whose own "worn clothing was so thin as to appear wholly unsuitable to the winter temperature"; like John Marvel, this stranger is alien to the more prosperous church he visits, and he is rebuffed by a wealthy churchgoer. The stranger, whose feet bleed from excessive exposure to the cold, is intended to suggest Christ in his selflessness. "The Stable of the Inn" is also religious, a specific retelling of the Golden Legend in which Page concentrates on the struggles of Joseph and Mary as they journey to Bethlehem. More contemporary is "The Shepherd Who Watched By Night"; like "The Stranger's Pew," this story considers a minister who is concerned more with the poor than with the outer trappings of the religion—the church and the ritual—and he is denigrated and scorned by materialistic parishioners. He has outlived his practical usefulness, but spiritually he still serves God: he helps to convert a dying prostitute; he aids a mother with her starving child.

There are variations on the same motives in other stories. In "The Bigot," a young minister opposes the spiritual rigidities of his Calvinist society and because of his conversion to the "birth of the heart," he loses his loved one and his position in the church. Since that time, he has "lived in exile—the exile of the heart" (167). In "The Outcast" a brilliant young lawyer lives a dissipated existence with a courtesan and is excluded from the best society. But he rises morally to become a stern, ethically puristic judge; he experiences retribution in the climax of the story when he presides over a case in which a prostitute kills a lover who has left her for a woman of his own class. The prostitute, without very much surprise to the reader, is the judge's own daughter.

Two other stories—"The Old Planter" and "The Trick-Doctor" —return to the subject of racial strife. In "The Old Planter,"

Northern drummers alter their attitudes toward an old Southern gentleman as they watch him courageously prevent a Negro from being lynched. The Negro has killed a man, but the Southern gentleman, once an aristocrat and a planter, arranges a fair trial. In "The Trick-Doctor," a "young city negro," who is a fraudulent preacher and a "trick-doctor," tries to dupe superstitious Negroes; but he is finally exposed and cast out by an old-time, faithful Negro and a white doctor.

The stories contained in *The Land of the Spirit*, Rosewell Page noted in 1923, "might have been written by Charles Kingsley, Dean Farrar, or Phillips Brooks." This statement is undoubtedly true, and it accounts for their mediocrity: not only is *The Land of the Spirit* filled with themes common to other contemporary writers but it does not modify Page's basic attitudes toward the Negro and religion. One can find similar anecdotes of the post-bellum Negro in *The Pastime Stories*, similar religious assumptions in *John Marvel, Assistant*. What is significant in both types of stories—and this observation holds true for *Gordon Keith, John Marvel, Assistant,* and the other stories that Page wrote in the twentieth century—is his tenacious insistence on the moral superiority of the past and his scorn of modern commercialism. "Riches," a character in one of these stories proclaims, "are the most sordid conception of the human intelligence" (230). Most of Page's fiction after *Red Rock*—the fiction considered in this chapter—is a dramatic rendering of that proclamation.

CHAPTER *6*

The Outer World

I N THE LAST TEN YEARS of his life, Page was a public figure. He wrote little and what he wrote—with the exception of *The Red Riders* (1924)—did not resemble his previous work. His time was spent in the political arena of Washington where he took an active interest in the presidential campaign of 1912. At the Democratic convention held in Baltimore, Page attempted to prevent Wilson's nomination and annoyed those Virginia Democrats who claimed Wilson as a native son. Page finally conceded by writing an open letter to the *New York Times* on October 27, 1912; and in the campaign of that year "he worked hard in his own state of Virginia to obtain" the election for Wilson. By January the two men were on close enough terms for the President, when "he came to Washington for his inauguration," to stay at Page's home.[1] In 1913 Virginia senators proposed Page as ambassador to Italy, and President Wilson appointed him. He served as ambassador from 1913 to 1919, devoting himself exclusively to political affairs, and he became friendly with various well-known people: the king and queen, and the sculptor, Sir Moses Ezekiel.

He developed a great affection for the Italian people, whose suffering in World War I moved him deeply. As an early observer noted, "there were many things in Italy's conduct during the war with which Mr. Page found fault; there were many times when he felt that his patience was wearing down, but never once did he fail to understand their point of view and endeavor to present it in all fairness to the President, and the State Department."[2] Personally, he "had used every effort within his power to get to know and be known by the Italians. Organized and managed by Mrs. Page and other American ladies, half the Embassy was turned into a supply base where materials sent from home were made into bandages and flannel clothes."[3] The Italians returned his affection: "Slowly it came into the minds of the Italian people that they had, in the person of the American Ambassador, a real friend on whom they could heavily lean in times of stress and trouble."[4] Few authors have enjoyed as much political and personal prestige in their later years as Page; and he lived long enough to offer his literary tribute to Italy, to write his version of the retreat from Caporetto.

I *Italy and Washington: Page as a Social Historian*

Upon his return to the United States, Page completed what was really a labor of love, *Italy and the World War* (1920). His intentions are clearly expressed in the preface to the book:

> . . . this work is divided into three parts. The first is introductory and contains in outline the History of the Italian People in the long period when they were included in and bound under the Holy Roman Empire. The second contains the story of their evolution, from the conception of their National Consciousness on through the long and bitter struggle with the Austrian Empire for their Liberty, down to the time when, under a Constitutional Sovereign, they developed into a new and United Italy, to become, almost at a bound, one of the Great Powers of Europe; yet with one step before her: the complete rounding out of her People, and the possession of her ancient strategic frontiers.
>
> The third part contains the story of the Diplomatic struggle to establish herself in a position to which Italy considered herself entitled as a Great Power and on which she has set what she believes her legitimate Aspirations, by virtue of her contribution to the World both in the Past and in this World War.
>
> What she performed in the War is related briefly that the Reader may know what one who was present in Italy throughout the War was able to learn on the spot of the part played therein by the Italian people.[5]

This long volume is full of interesting, informative commentary, but regretfully it makes no reference to Page's own experiences at the time. What it does indicate is his sympathetic commitment to the Italian people, a commitment that is reflected in his idealization of the Italians' role in the war. The emphasis, for the most part, is on the Italian people and their heroism in the war. Compared with Hemingway's dramatic version of the conflict in *A Farewell to Arms, Italy and the World War* is naturally less immediate and powerful—it reads more like a text than the work of a serious artist. But what is interesting, in terms of literary history, is the difference in the attitudes of both authors. Page expresses an automatic adulation; Hemingway, a deep disillusionment that grows out of his personal involvement in the war.

Italy and the World War was written in Santa Barbara, California, in the winter of 1919-1920. Page returned to Virginia in 1920, but he did not remain there. In October, his daughter fell ill, and he sailed to England to be with her. After she had recovered, he traveled to the Riviera to rest for the winter and did not return to the United States until 1921. In October of that year he went to the Midwest—to Denver and Pueblo—where he delivered various lectures, one of them traditional, "The South's Contribution to the West," but others that reflect an interest in Dante, the poet whom he had grown to admire more than any other.

These literary lectures were collected in a book that Page published in 1922, *Dante and His Influence*. "In presenting this study of Dante Alighieri," he writes in the introduction to this short volume, "I would not claim that I can add anything new to the vast volume of interpretation which devotion and scholarship have, at least in Italy, piled during these six hundred years— and more recently in other countries—about his revered name. All that is even pretended is to present in succinct form a brief sketch of the Poet of Poets and of the conditions amid which that life was cast."[6] The book that follows is similar to many literary studies that were written by nineteenth-century American authors; Page concentrates on Dante's life and its historical background, devoting only a chapter to a general appreciation of *The Divine Comedy*. He succeeds in achieving his limited goal of writing an impressionistic, laudatory account of Dante and his times and of doing "honor to Italy and her greatest poet."[7]

In the same year he wrote another, entirely different work, *Washington and Its Romance* (1923), in which he pays tribute to the city where he had lived and prospered since 1893. The book is admittedly romantic:

> The capitals of most countries are the especial pride of their people [he writes in the introduction]. It is not so with us—at least, it has not been so in the past. Happily, it appears as though

this condition were changing. It has, indeed, ever appeared to me strange that Americans know so little of and care so little for the capital of their own country. Nature, prodigal of gracious slope and curve and tone has endowed it with, perhaps, more charm than any other national capital—at least, than any large European capital—and its founders laid it off on a generous plan which has left the opportunity of furthering what Nature presented, in a way to appeal to the pride of our people.[8]

Functioning as a social historian, Page writes of "The Planning of the Capital," the "Early Social Life in Washington," and "Jefferson's Administration," and offers a historical account, a traditional and affectionate report of the capital city.

II The Red Riders

In May, 1921, Page had made a visit to South Carolina with his brother Rosewell to "refresh his memory as to the scenes and incidents of the Hampton 'Red Shirt Campaign.'"[9] Page was resuming a sequel to *Red Rock* that he had begun as early as 1900. "I intend to write some day," he had told a friend in 1900, "another novel based on the uprising in 1876. This is one of the most picturesque incidents in our history. I have already done some work on this."[10] The novel was originally entitled *The Sabine Farm,* and he was working on the manuscript at his death; his brother wrote the last few sections and published the volume posthumously in 1924.[11]

More than forty years had passed since Reconstruction; more than twenty years had intervened since the publication of *Red Rock*. But *The Red Riders* does not gain objectivity—in spite of the fact that it is set in South Carolina rather than in Virginia—and it lacks the sense of commitment, the passionate anguish that gives the earlier novel a powerful immediacy. Furthermore, Page makes no real distinction between Reconstruction in South Carolina and in Virginia: the desperate conditions of the post-bellum people, the horrors of Black Reconstruction, the scurrility of the scalawags and carpetbaggers are identical, and The Red Riders, who are introduced at the end of the novel, are merely equivalents of the Ku Klux Klan.

Other aspects of *The Red Riders* remind the reader of *Red Rock*. On a small pre-Civil War plantation, a place that is "a world in itself," young Sinkler Ashley matures. Like the youthful heroes of *Red Rock*, Ashley is extremely chauvinistic and completely dedicated to the code of Southern heroism. After a visit to the city, where he is impressed by the nobility of President Lincoln and enlightened as to the moral turpitude of a Republican senator, he returns to his home, prepared to defend South Carolina against hostile invaders. Surrounding Ashley are the familiar trappings of Reconstruction: the wild, insurgent freedmen and the suffering whites; the pious and innocent Northern teacher—a lady abolitionist—who unwittingly buys a plantation from an avaricious scalawag; the faithful Negro slaves who refuse to take their freedom. "I was born 'pon dis plantation," one Negro scolds his master, "and I has lived here de length of man's allotted days, an' I seed three ginerations come and go right here, and I has always considered it my home and I still considers it so."[12]

This novel has no clear movement and is really an arrangement of familiar situations. The most familiar situation emerges at the end of the book when Sinkler Ashley marries a Northern girl; Reconstruction is over and the marriage, which symbolizes sectional reconciliation, suggests the strengthening of a new Union. The one original characteristic of the novel, promised by the romantic title, is the introduction of the Red Riders. This group arises late in the Reconstruction period; and, according to Page, it is purely defensive. It opposes the Freedmen's Bureau, hostile Negroes, the Radical Republicans and scalawags; specifically, it attempts to maintain honest voting regulations. "'Do you think this action of the Red Shirts justifiable?' asked a member of the opposite party of Ashley before a congressional investigation committee months afterward." And the hero answers: "'It saved the civilization of a part of the United States which had helped to create them. It was revolutionary. It was only justifiable as any revolution is justifiable,' Ashley replied."[13]

The Red Riders are entirely successful; at the end of the book, the hero is able to exclaim: "South Carolina is herself again. She is in the hands of her own people—redeemed and disenthralled —Hampton is governor—no matter who is President. You [the Red Riders] have done it."[14] Sectional reconciliation has been achieved in the marriage of Diane McQuair and Sinkler Ashley; but it is the "reconciliation" that the reader is now familiar with in Page's fiction—a capitulation and conversion to Southern standards. The Republicans are defeated; the Negroes return to their proper role as servants; the lady abolitionist admits her foolish errand. In the late nineteenth-century, this literary propaganda dominated the magazines, and one can understand it, at least historically; but *The Red Riders* was written a year before Page's death and was publilshed posthumously by his brother. In 1924 it seems like a manuscript left over from another generation.

III *The Epitaph of a Civilization*

"Thomas Nelson Page had an ideal life,"[15] wrote Rosewell Page in 1923, one year after his brother's death. That judgment is substantially correct, although one would naturally modify it in terms of such a tragedy as the youthful death of his first wife. Page enjoyed a full and varied life, and he achieved the affluence and prestige he so desired. In the "renaissance of the South," he became an acclaimed literary spokcsman, not only in his fiction but also in the addresses he delivered throughout the country. As a leading figure in Washington society during the 1890's and the early twentieth century, he enjoyed wide popularity and a measure of political influence. As ambassador to Italy from 1913 to 1919, he achieved international fame and the deep respect of the Italian people.

His literary career was still more ideal than his life—as ideal as that of any author with his limited talents. He came to the writing of fiction when, in the words of a Southern critic, "the South had no chronicler and found itself arraigned at the bar of the world without . . . defense."[16] Page took up this challenge with chauvinistic determination and offered a complete defense of Southern life before the war, of the white man's relationship with the Negro. His countless stories and essays form one of the clearest, most powerful statements of white supremacy in nineteenth-century Southern literature. He did not hesitate to add an optimistic and sentimental coloring of the imagination to all that he wrote; so idealized were his memories of the old régime, in fact, that he could not see it in any other way even when he assumed the role of historian. He attributed a heroism and courage to his Southern gentlemen and ladies, a loyalty to his Negro slaves, that was extreme and often offensive; but in stories like "Marse Chan," "Meh Lady," and "Unc' Edinburg's Drowndin'," his idealized vision was perfectly suited to the sentimental tale that he rendered: these figures are actors in the great drama of a vanished civilization, and his exaggerations are those of myth and legend.

Artistically, the stories of *In Ole Virginia* are superb; they are minor classics of their type, distinct and unique like all memorable fiction, and they remain among the great stories of American literature. It is true, as F. L. Pattee points out, that "like the rest of his school" Page "mistook the voice of his decade [the 1880's] for the voice of permanence and poured out in profusion what the decade desired"; it is also true that "he was too much dominated by his materials," that "his novels become treatises, source books, defenses of the Southern position, picture books."[17] But "Marse Chan," "Unc' Edinburg's Drowndin'," and "Meh Lady" evoke a world nowhere else described so elaborately or so exquisitely. They capture and raise to a level of high lyric emotion the sundry characteristics of the code of heroism that one can trace through nineteenth-century Southern fiction, and their appearance in the 1880's "stands as the high-water mark of the local color flood," as one of the culminating gestures of the sentimental approach to life and literature and history. In Thomas Nelson Page's fiction, with all its varied merits and defects, one finds an accurate mirror of one dominant aspect of nineteenth-century Southern literature.

Ideal also was Page's critical reception. Politically, the nation was eager for tales of reconciliation. The Civil War was over, and readers wanted to know of heroism and not sectional strife, of the mutual admiration of Northern and Southern warriors and not the actual rancor that often existed. Page rarely reminds his readers of the specific facts of ante-bellum life or of the Reconstruction; his technique is to blur the historical picture and to create moral contrasts that always transcend individual bitter conflicts. The heroes may be Northerners as well as Southerners, for the criterion of moral behavior is not sectional, not political, but personal and hereditary: the great question is whether the fictional figure is a gentleman. Edwin Mims was justified in remarking, at the turn of the century, that Page was influential in "the fostering of the new national spirit"[18] which had been so characteristic of the late nineteenth century. Once he had impressed his picture of plantation life on the national imagination, he found himself able to publish his work in important journals like *Scribner's Monthly, Harper's New Monthly*

Magazine, *The North American Review,* and *The Atlantic Monthly;* and he discovered that he could publish anything he wrote. In a period from April, 1892, until February, 1894, for example, no month passed without a sketch or story or essay by Page in the magazines. Almost all of them were concerned with racial issues, and many of them were hastily written and artistically inferior.

In an age when critical standards were not especially high, Page enjoyed favorable commentaries on even the poorer stories of the 1890's; and his work appealed enormously to the popular reader. *Red Rock,* according to Rosewell Page, sold more than one thousand copies and ranked fifth in a list of best sellers;[19] *Gordon Keith* was second on a similar list of 1903. It was not until 1906, in fact, that he had real difficulty in publishing anything he wrote. "By the way," he complained to Robert Underwood Johnson on December 22, 1906, "if you wish me ever to send anything else that I write except my Jamestown sketch to the *Century,* be good enough to tell me where is the dividing line between a story and a sketch. I mean, of course, a sufficiently vivid sketch. This is the second piece of writing on paper that I have sent to the *Century* under the impression that it was a good story, which has been stamped sketch and returned . . . I do not know just what constitutes the difference."[20] It was not until August, 1907, that a critic wrote of his "waning influence" in a direct and unsentimental fashion. "He delineated the immortal features of a heartbroken people in terms of personality sufficiently graceful and heroic to satisfy this lofty sense they had of themselves. The kind of mind he has is sensitized not to facts, but to the poetry of facts. . . . But the fact remains that the South has outgrown Mr. Page one way or the other. The spirit of the South dramatized in his books is no longer sufficiently related to this new spirit to command its interest and obeisance."[21]

By 1907 Page had seen the local-color movement surrender to a more realistic treatment of life in literature; and, with the exception of *The Red Riders,* he did not write extensively of the South again. He had become, in his own lifetime, the creator of "the Virginia classic," and few authors could have hoped for more favorable estimations of their most important work. He was praised not only by the popular press but by most critics and scholars of Southern literature. Charles W. Coleman, in a comprehensive and typical essay of its kind, "The Recent Movement in Southern Literature" (1887), noted in regard to "Marse Chan" that "Mr. Page enjoys the reputation of having written the most exquisite story of the war that has yet appeared."[22] In 1913 Edwin Mims, one of the first professional scholars of Southern literature, concluded that "Hawthorne was not better adapted to the delineation of New England Puritanism or Scott to the setting forth of the age of chivalry, than was Mr. Page to the description and interpretation of ante-bellum life."[23]

George W. Cable, who differed radically from Page in his solutions to the race problem, referred to the Virginian as "the author of those beautiful stories of Old Virginia, and of those lofty pleadings for the nobler civic and social relics of the old South, which have made him famous and shown the sincerity and ardor of his patriotism as citizen of a whole America."[24] Finally, Arthur Hobson Quinn, a scholar who recognized from the outset Page's special contribution to American literature, wrote in 1909: "In the renaissance of the South, Thomas Nelson Page played a most prominent part, not only in his poems, his novels and his short stories, but also in the addresses he had made throughout the country, in which he deals directly with Southern life and character. . . . The quality which makes these short stories great is the surety with which the effect is reached."[25]

Since his death Page has received less than ideal treatment by most critics; he has either been ignored or relegated to a footnote as one of the important local colorists. But his work deserves more extensive examination. Historically, his fiction reveals the typical attitudes of the Southern conservative and offers a point of view that is still very real in American politics and life today. By understanding his reasons for idealizing the old South and by making distinctions between his idealized version and reality, the modern reader can begin to understand the roots of racial problems—the beginnings of hostility between Negro and white in the South. The code of heroism that Page assigns his most sympathetic figures is "bred in the bone"; more than any other Southern writer of the nineteenth century, he explores the full significance of that code. Works like *In Ole Virginia, Social Life in Old Virginia,* and *The Negro: the Southerner's Problem* are an immediate revelation of the major assumptions that many nineteenth-century Southerners made.

Esthetically, Page is of less significance. Most of his fiction is burdened by traditional sentimentality, by a rigid point of view that causes him to polarize the various character types in his work. "My design," he explained, "is to picture Life as it appeals to me and as it appears to me, and to show that whatever the hardships may be, it is after all worth living."[26] Consequently, most of his heroes are heroic beyond belief and his villains are ludicrous contrasts, the stock types of popular romance. In fiction like *Gordon Keith* and *John Marvel, Assistant,* where the locale is not the South and the subject is not the death of ante-bellum civilization, Page is as maudlin and predictable as most sentimental writers; in *Red Rock* and other works which deal with the post-bellum South and racial problems, he yields too easily to the formula of reconciliation; he converts his tales into tendentious propaganda that is often artistically inorganic.

From all that he wrote—from the great number of essays and novels, stories and sketches, poems, plays, and addresses—there remain a few minor masterpieces: "Marse Chan," "Unc' Edinburg's Drowndin'," "Meh Lady," and "Ole 'Stracted." These poignant tales offer a unique, memorable vision of idealized plantation life in the ante-bellum South at the moment of its decline. As such they are "the epitaph of a civilization,"[27] and they belong among the small but original achievements in American literature.

Notes and References

Preface

1. Grace King, *Grace King: Memories of A Southern Woman of Letters* (New York, 1932), p. 377.
2. Thomas Nelson Page, *The Novels, Stories, Sketches, and Poems of Thomas Nelson Page*. The Plantation Edition. (New York, 1906-1912), I, xi. Hereafter just the volume and page numbers will be given, and they will be incorporated in the text. Only those books and essays that do not appear in the Plantation Edition are listed in these notes and references.
3. Arlin Turner (ed.), *Southern Stories* (New York, 1960), p. xx.

Chapter One

1. Rosewell Page, *Thomas Nelson Page, A Memoir of a Virginia Gentleman* (New York, 1923), p. 2.
2. Harriet Holman, *The Literary Career of Thomas Nelson Page, 1884-1910* (unpublished Ph.D dissertation, Duke University, 1947), p. 3. The biographical information here and elsewhere is drawn for the most part from Miss Holman's dissertation. But see also Rosewell Page's biography; Page's own essays in *The Old Dominion;* A. C. Gordon's *Virginian Portraits* (Staunton, 1924); *Dictionary of American Biography* (New York, 1934), XIV, 141-42; Susan Pendleton Lee, *Memoirs of William Nelson Pendleton, D. D.* (Philadelphia, 1893); *Encyclopedia of Virginia Biography*.
3. Holman, p. 11.
4. VIII, 140, Dedication to *Santa Claus's Partner*.
5. Quoted in Holman, p. 13.
6. *Ibid.*, p. 16.
7. This incident is reported by A. C. Gordon in "Thomas Nelson Page: An Appreciation," *Scribner's Magazine*, LXXIII (January, 1923), 79, and reprinted in *Virginian Portraits*. A full account follows:

"In these early years one of his college intimates, then living in Charlottesville, got a commission from a New York newspaper to 'report' an address that Ralph Waldo Emerson had accepted an invitation to make at the university, and Page came up on a similar errand for a Richmond daily. Mr. Emerson was then quite an old man, and the lecture was delivered in so low a tone that few heard it. The two young 'reporters,' when it was concluded, approached him with the deference due his age and reputation, and prayed the temporary loan of his manuscript. He replied that he 'wanted nothing to do with them—that he was at war with newspaper reporters' and refused the proffered request. The disappointed youths, the value of whose reports depended entirely on what they might give of the sage of Concord's essay, retired in high dudgeon, and together concocted a letter to the Richmond paper which dealt with Mr. Emerson in a manner not at all complimentary. The article appeared next day in the paper, and created consternation among the university authorities who threatened to debar the offenders thenceforth from the precincts. The matter, however, was soon forgotten. . . ."

See also Hubert H. Hoeltje, "Emerson in Virginia," *New England Quarterly*, V (October, 1932), 753-68.

8. Quoted in Holman, p. 25.

9. Quoted in Carl Holliday, *A History of Southern Literature* (New York, 1906), p. 309.

10. Holman, p. 50.

11. Rollin Gustav Osterweis, *Romanticism and Nationalism in the Old South* (New Haven, 1949), pp. 55, 94, 54-102 *passim*.

12. I, ix. Miss Holman believes that " 'Marse Chan' developed from a letter shown Page by either Armistead Churchill Gordon or some mutual friend." Page wrote a slightly different account of this experience in a letter to William Malone Baskervill: "Just then a friend showed me a letter which had been written by a young girl to her sweetheart in a Georgia regiment, telling him that she had discovered that she loved him, after all, and that if he would get a furlough and come home she would marry him; that she had loved him ever since they had gone to school together in the little schoolhouse in the woods. Then, as if she feared such a temptation might be too strong for him, she added a postscript in these words: 'Don't come without a furlough; for if you don't come honorable, I won't marry you.' This letter had been taken from the pocket of a private dead on the battlefield of one of the battles around Richmond, and as the date was only a week or two before the battle occurred, its pathos struck me very much. I remember I said: 'The poor fellow got his furlough through a bullet.' The idea remained with me, and I went to my office one morning and began to write 'Marse Chan,' which was finished in about a week." Edwin Mims, "Thomas Nelson Page," *Southern Writers*, II (Nashville, 1903), 134-35.

13. I, x. The story was revised before it was published in 1884. "Early in 1881 an unnamed member of the staff of *Scribner's Monthly*" wrote to Page: "We like the story and will print it, on the condition that some omissions may be made toward the first part.

It is good but some of it is extraneous to the subject of the story which we take to be the relations of the young couple. Either you or we could make these omissions which we are sure would add to the unity and force of impression of the whole. We enclose our check in payment for the MS." Letter to Thomas Nelson Page, January 1, 1881, quoted in Holman, p. 55.

In 1925, Robert Underwood Johnson noted that "Marse Chan" had "but one fault, that of redundancy, the action being retarded by a surplusage of interesting detail. . . . With the consent of the author, excision was made of this disgressive material—perhaps a third of the original material. . . . The magazine had already on its accepted list a number of admirable examples of such stories [in dialect] by well-known writers and the obligation of precedence and not a lack of appreciation of the tale itself, was the occasion of the delay of its publication for nearly three years." Robert Underwood Johnson, "Thomas Nelson Page," *Commemorative Tributes,* American Academy of Arts and Letters, Academy Publication No. 50, pp. 2-3.

14. Holman, p. 160.

15. See *The Nation,* XLV (September 22, 1881), 236, for a similar observation. Jay B. Hubbell in *Southern Life in Fiction* (Athens, 1960), p. 85, makes the pointed remark that too many Southern authors "shared the old slaveholder's defensive attitude that the Negroes cared little or nothing about freedom."

16. Arthur Hobson Quinn, *American Fiction, An Historical and Critical Survey* (New York, 1936), p. 357.

17. Jay B. Hubbell, *Virginia Life in Fiction, American Literature* (New York, 1922), pp. 28, 29.

18. *Ibid.,* p. 27.

19. Turner, pp. xxi-xxii.

20. Francis P. Gaines, *The Southern Plantation, A Study in the Development and the Accuracy of a Tradition* (New York, 1924), p. 78.

21. Quinn, p. 358.

22. Paul H. Buck, *The Road to Reunion* (New York, 1959), p. 224.

23. Meh Lady is apparently modeled after Page's first wife. The Negroes are also patterned after actual people: "Old Hannah" was suggested by the Mammy of the Page household; and Uncle Balla, the carriage driver, was modeled after Ralph, the servant of Page's father.

24. Quinn, p. 357.

25. Buck, p. 214. Buck goes on to point out that "there was not an important writer of" the Southern school of local color "who did not believe the South better off within the restored Union."

26. Rosewell Page, p. 202.

27. Holman, p. 69.

28. John T. Trowbridge, *My Own Story* (New York, 1903), pp. 310-11.

29. Hubbell, *Virginia Life in Fiction*, p. 29.

30. Mims, II, 140.

31. Albion W. Tourgée, "The South as a Field for Fiction," *The Forum*, VI (December, 1888), 405.

Chapter Two

1. Quoted in Holman, p. 28.

2. In a letter to Miss Mildred Lewis Rutherford, teacher of literature at the Lucy Cobb Institute in Athens, Georgia, Page wrote: "Any mention of me, however, [for a forthcoming edition of American Authors] would be incomplete without giving proper credit to my lovely wife, who was my inspiration and my model and for whom I wrote and whose memory is now my most cherished possession." Quoted in William M. E. Rachal, "Some Letters of Thomas Nelson Page," *The Virginia Magazine of History and Biography*, 61 (April, 1953), 180.

3. See Gordon, p. 79.

4. Charles W. Kent, "Thomas Nelson Page," *South Atlantic Quarterly*, V (July, 1907), 264.

5. See also Page's preface to George W. Bagby, *The Old Virginia and Other Sketches* (New York, 1911), p. x, for an astute estimation of pre-war writers.

6. Page, "Literature in the South Since the War," *Lippincott's Magazine*, XLVIII (December, 1891), 742, 755.

7. XII, p. 189. See Hubbell, *Southern Life in Fiction*, for a brief history of the gentleman in Southern fiction.

8. Hubbell, *Virginia Life in Fiction*, pp. 28-29, 53-54.

9. *Ibid.*, pp. 27-28.

10. Quoted in Thomas Nelson Page, *The Negro: The Southerner's Problem* (New York, 1910), p. 217. Further page references to this volume will be incorporated in the text. This essay was originally included in *The Old South* (1892) and is the one article of that volume which Page chose to exclude from The Plantation Edition. Perhaps he felt that its arguments were too extreme. He wanted to be remembered as the author of reconciliation and, as a consequence, he also deleted *The Negro: The Southerner's Problem* from his Collected Works.

11. Holman, p. 103.

12. *Ibid.*, p. 101.

13. Page, *The Negro: The Southerner's Problem*, p. 302.

14. Rayford Logan, *The Negro in American Life and Thought. The Nadir 1877-1901* (New York, 1954), pp. 35, 37.

15. Buck, pp. 243-44.
16. *Ibid.*, p. 244.
17. Tourgée, "The South as a Field for Fiction," p. 405.
18. Gaines, p. 78.
19. Edmund Wilson, *Patriotic Gore: Studies in the Literature of the American Civil War* (New York, 1962), pp. 613-14.
20. Holman, p. 73.
21. Quinn, pp. 358-59.

Chapter Three

1. Quinn, p. 360. Compare this statement with a long and complete explanation that Page wrote to Henry Simms Hartzog, President of Clemson College, February 4, 1900: "I intended 'Red Rock' for a 'composite picture,' as you phrase it, or rather, I intended it for a picture that would stand for the south generally under the conditions that prevailed in reconstruction times, rather than only for Virginia. The characters, perhaps, are more Virginian than those of other States, as I know the Virginian character best; though I believe the same types existed in other States as well as in Virginia. But the conditions, particularly those relating to the K. K. K. were such as prevailed in more southern States. The incident of the wholesale arrest was taken from the history of South Carolina, as recorded in Prof. Leland's book, 'A Voice from South Carolina.' The conditions in South Carolina were so dreadful as scarcely to bear relation, the country would hardly believe it now, so for purposes of art I had to 'tone' them down. Even as I wrote the story many people think I grossly overstated the case, and I get many letters asking for my authorities. To all these I say: read the history of South Carolina.

"I intend to write some day another novel based on the uprising in 1876. This is one of the most picturesque incidents in our history. I have already done some work on this." Quoted in Holman, pp. 76-77. The book Page alludes to is *The Sabine Farm*, renamed *The Red Riders*.

2. IV, xi. The model for Miss Thomasia was Page's Aunt Rose.

3. "Recent Novels," *Nation*, LXVIII (March 2, 1899), 167.

4. See, for example, Arthur Hobson Quinn, "Mr. Page in Fiction and Poetry," *Book News Monthly*, XXVIII (November, 1909), 144.

5. Hubbell, *Southern Life in Fiction*, pp. 84-85.

6. Page to Henry Simms Hartzog, February 4, 1900, quoted in Holman, p. 76.

7. See H. L. Swint, *The Northern Teacher in the South, 1862-1870* (Nashville, 1941), pp. 135-63.

8. V, 179. Tourgée makes use of the same situation in *Bricks Without Straw* (New York, 1880), p. 256. Contemporary Southern

readers objected violently to Blair Cary's teaching a school for colored children. "It was a circumstance unheard of except in *Red Rock* and 'Meh Lady,' declared a troubled Memphis admirer, and to settle a wager another reader asked whether Page knew of a case 'in real life of a young lady in the south occupying the social position' of Blair Cary and teaching Negroes in public school. Page evidently answered with names and places, but such incidents were incredible to people in some sections of the South." Holman, p. 77.

9. Henry W. Lanier, "Fiction, Poetry, and the Lighter Note in the Season's Books," *American Monthly Review of Reviews,* XXV (December, 1898), 725; "Red Rock," *Athenaeum,* CXIII (February 11, 1899), 176. See also "Recent Novels," *Nation,* LXVIII (March 2, 1899), 166-68; "Red Rock, A Chronicle of Reconstruction," *Critic,* XXXIV (January, 1899), 83-84; "Some Recent Fiction," *Atlantic Monthly,* LXXXIII (April, 1899), 519-20; and Holman, pp. 79-86, *passim.*

10. Note two typical reactions to Red Rock: "*Red Rock* fixes upon a permanent canvas a picture of a vanished civilization and a national crime" in a much better way "than any historical treatist could do. . . . What impresses the reader most is the author's restraint. With his traditions and sympathies, he might have been pardoned if he had laid the colors on more thickly, but he has preferred writing a novel to a political tract." Quinn, "Mr. Page in Fiction and Poetry," p. 144.

Edwin Mims writes: "*Red Rock* as a novel is not equal to his best short stories,—in plot and incident it is not satisfying,—but that it is a successful historical romance and the most faithful reproduction of that stormy period is open to little doubt. It is accurate, fair, restrained. The author's discrimination between various types of Northerners, Southerners, and negroes is worthy of the highest praise. It stands out in striking contrast with the melodramatic and sensational novels that have been recently written on that period. There is naught of malice in it." Mims, II, 115.

Chapter Four

1. Holman, p. 44.
2. Page to William Hamilton Hayne, Richmond, December 13, 1887, Hayne mss. Quoted in Holman, p. 67.
3. Holman, p. 91.
4. Quinn, "Mr. Page in Fiction and Poetry," p. 144.
5. Page, *The Coast of Bohemia* (New York, 1906), pp. v-vi.
6. Wilson, p. 607.
7. Page, *The Negro: The Southerner's Problem,* p. 7. Further page references to this volume will be incorporated in the text.

Chapter Five

1. See "Gordon Keith," *Athenaeum* (August 29, 1902), p. 281; "Mr. Page's Novel," *Independent*, LV (August 20, 1903), 1993-1994; "Bret Harte and Sundry Novels," *The Nation*, LXXVII (August 6, 1903), 118.

2. Quoted in "The Waning Influence of Thomas Nelson Page," *Current Opinion*, XLII (August, 1907), 172.

3. Holman, p. 66.

4. "On the Decay of Manners," *Century Magazine*, LXXXI (April, 1911), 881-87.

5. "A Goth," according to Miss Holman, was based on the character of John Fox, Jr., a friend of Page who was an incorrigible gambler and drinker. The original version of the story was called "The Gambler," but Page changed the title and locale so as not to embarrass or offend his friend.

6. Note Page's own comments on this story: "I think . . . 'Leander's Light,' a pretty good relation, I mean for me, of minor events in the life of an old Maine countryman and his sister. It was written with a view to showing that under their hard and repellent exterior there lies a deep vein of sentiment that makes them close kin to the rest of Anglo-Saxondom, to whom love of home and family is the most vital and lasting of all principles." Page to Robert Underwood Johnson, December 22, 1900. Quoted in Holman, p. 151.

7. The reaction of John Fox to this story is interesting: "I've just read 'My Friend—the Doctor.' It's a bully story and you are certainly surprising in your power of brief vivid characterization. Again, too, the breadth of your intellectual sympathies astonishes me. But I felt about it as about the Goth—that you are recklessly squandering themes and characters. There isn't a character in 'The Doctor' that isn't strong enough to go on through a big novel with no further description or analysis—and the Goth alone was big enough to carry the weight of a book. Gee, my storehouse (or rather doll's house) of ideas and fiction-people couldn't stand any such drain as you are giving yours. . . . Lordy, man, put 'em in a novel." John Fox to Page, October 31, 1907. Quoted in Holman, p. 161.

8. XV, 13-14. Rosewell Page notes, in regard to Wolffert, that "the young Jew, perhaps, is the hero of the story. It is interesting to recall the fact that when the book appeared a member of a distinguished body of Jews, which met in Washington, presented those in attendance with a copy of the book, containing the author's autograph, which had been so signed at the donor's request. A young Hebrew friend of his in Richmond gave to the author many of the ideas with which he has endowed 'Wolfert.'" Rosewell Page, pp. 203-4.

9. See as typical a letter from Cyrus Adler to Page: "Barring Leo Levy, the Jews that I know well that you know at all, are all people of ordinary earth, but possibly inheriting exceptional intellectual traditions and forced into a seeming idealism by the momentary misery of their race and of the human race. However I shall not quarrel with you if you wish to believe well of us and even if you believe too well of me." Cyrus Adler to Page, October 19, 1909. Quoted in Holman, p. 128.

10. Rosewell Page, p. 203.

11. Hubbell, *Virginia Life in Fiction*, p. 37.

12. Quinn, "Mr. Page in Fiction and Poetry," p. 144.

13. Page, *The Land of the Spirit* (New York, 1913), pp. v-vi. Other page references to this volume are incorporated in the text.

Chapter Six

1. Ronald Tree, "Thomas Nelson Page," *Forum*, LXIX (January, 1923), 1137-42. A new collection of Page's correspondence has been presented by Page's step-grandson to the College of William and Mary. These letters—305 in number—reflect upon Page's life and career during the period covered in this chapter.

2. *Ibid.*, p. 1137.

3. *Ibid.*, p. 1141.

4. *Ibid.*, p. 1142.

5. Page, *Italy and the World War* (New York, 1920), pp. viii-ix.

6. Page, *Dante and His Influence* (New York, 1922), p. xiii.

7. *Ibid.*, p. 238.

8. Page, *Washington and Its Romance* (New York, 1923), pp. ix-x.

9. Rosewell Page, p. 178.

10. Page to Henry Simms Hartzog, February 4, 1900. Quoted in Holman, p. 77.

11. "On the basis of style and structure," Miss Holman surmises, "it seems probably that Page wrote most of the volume just after the publication of *Red Rock* and that Rosewell wrote pp. 308-38 from his brother's notes. It is a section so compressed that it may have been intended as a second volume." Holman, p. 77.

12. Thomas Nelson Page, *The Red Riders* (New York, 1924), p. 91.

13. *Ibid.*, p. 318.

14. *Ibid.*, pp. 333-34.

15. Rosewell Page, p. 205.

16. Mims, II, 140.

17. Fred Lewis Pattee, *The Development of the American Short Story* (New York, 1923), p. 285.

18. Mims, II, pp. 150-51.

19. See also Alice Payne Hackett, *Fifty Years of Best Sellers, 1895-1945* (New York, 1948), p. 15.

20. Quoted in Holman, p. 151.

21. Quoted in "The Waning Influence of Thomas Nelson Page, *Current Opinion*, XLIII (August, 1907), 171-72.

22. Charles W. Coleman Jr., "The Recent Movement in Southern Literature," *Harper's New Monthly Magazine*, LXXIV (May, 1887), 848.

23. Edwin Mims, "Thomas Nelson Page," *Atlantic Monthly*, L (July, 1907), 112.

24. George W. Cable, "Thomas Nelson Page, a Study in Reminiscence and Appreciation," *The Book News Monthly*, XVII (November, 1909), 140, 141. Page's comments on Cable, eighteen years earlier, are equally complimentary: "These pictures [in *Ole Creole Days*] may thus not be true to Creole life, but they rise into the high plane of ideality; they are true to human life. . . . The writer reprobates Mr. Cable's theories of political-social economy as unsound and unsafe, but he will never cease to be proud that, whatever direction Mr. Cable's philosophy may assume, his literary genius is the offspring of the South." Page, "Literature in the South Since the War," pp. 747-48.

25. Quinn, "Mr. Page in Fiction and Poetry," pp. 142, 143.

26. Quoted in Holman, p. 155.

27. Rosewell Page, p. 88.

Selected Bibliography

PRIMARY SOURCES

A fuller bibliography may be found in Harriet Holman's useful doctoral dissertation, *The Literary Career of Thomas Nelson Page, 1884-1910*. Whereas I list only the original publication date of books, Miss Holman adds later editions. Furthermore, she includes various contemporaneous reviews of Page's published books; most of these reviews have little value—they are, for the most part, impressionistic and cursory—but they do suggest the general acceptance of Page's vision of the South.

In addition to Miss Holman's dissertation, a new collection of correspondence, photographs, and documents is now available at the College of William and Mary. Page's step-grandson, Dr. Henry Field, has presented to the library 305 items, most of which reflect upon Page's life and career during the period that he was United States Ambassador to Italy.

Starred items indicate that the book or article is not included in the Plantation Edition. A fairly extensive listing of Page's articles is offered so that the reader who has no access to the Plantation Edition can easily find the material he wants.

1. Books

Address. Washington: West Virginia Mining Association, 1910.

Address at the Three Hundredth Anniversary of the Settlement of Jamestown. Richmond: Whittet and Shepperson, 1919.

Among the Camps; or, Young People's Stories of the War. New York: Charles Scribner's Sons, 1891.

Befo' de War: Echoes in Negro Dialect. A. C. GORDON, joint author. New York: Charles Scribner's Sons, 1888.

Bred in the Bone. New York: Charles Scribner's Sons, 1904.

The Burial of the Guns, and Other Stories. New York: Charles Scribner's Sons, 1894.

A Captured Santa Claus. New York: Charles Scribner's Sons, 1902.

The Coast of Bohemia. New York: Charles Scribner's Sons, 1906.

Dante and His Influence. New York: Charles Scribner's Sons, 1922.

Elsket, and Other Stories. New York: Charles Scribner's Sons, 1891.

Gordon Keith. New York: Charles Scribner's Sons, 1903.

In Ole Virginia; or, Marse Chan and Other Stories. New York: Charles Scribner's Sons, 1887.

*_Italy and the World War._ New York: Charles Scribner's Sons, 1920.

John Marvel, Assistant. New York: Charles Scribner's Sons, 1909.

*_The Land of the Spirit._ New York: Charles Scribner's Sons, 1913.

*_The Loss of the Fiduciary Principle._ Albany: New York State Bar Association, 1907.

Marse Chan: A Story of Old Virginia. New York: Charles Scribner's Sons, 1900.

Meh Lady: A Story of the War. New York: Charles Scribner's Sons, 1900.

*_Mount Vernon and Its Preservation, 1858-1910._ New York: Knickerbocker Press, 1910.

*_The Negro: The Southerner's Problem._ New York: Charles Scribner's Sons, 1904.

The Novels, Stories, Sketches and Poems of Thomas Nelson Page. The Plantation Edition. New York: Charles Scribner's Sons, 1906-1912. 18 volumes.

The Old Dominion: Her Making and Her Manners. New York: Charles Scribner's Sons, 1908.

The Old Gentleman of the Black Stock. New York: Charles Scribner's, 1897.

The Old South: Essays Social and Political. New York: Charles Scribner's Sons, 1892.

On Newfound River. New York: Charles Scribner's Son, 1891.

*_The Page Story Book._ Edited by FRANK E. SPAULDING and CATHERINE T. BRYCE. New York: Charles Scribner's Sons, 1906.

Pastime Stories. New York: Harper and Brothers, 1894.

*_The Peace Cross Book,_ Cathedral of SS. Peter and Paul, Washington. New York: R. H. Russell, 1899.

Polly: A Christmas Recollection. New York: Charles Scribner's Sons, 1894.

*_The Red Riders._ New York: Charles Scribner's Sons, 1924.

Red Rock: A Chronicle of Reconstruction. New York: Charles Scribner's Sons, 1898.

Robert E. Lee, Man and Soldier. New York: Charles Scribner's Sons, 1911.

*_Robert E. Lee, Southerner._ New York: Charles Scribner's Sons, 1908.

Santa Claus's Partner. New York: Charles Scribner's Sons, 1899.

Social Life in Old Virginia. New York: Charles Scribner's Sons, 1897.

*_The Shepherd Who Watched by Night._ New York: Charles Scribner's Sons, 1913.

*_The Stranger's Pew._ New York: Charles Scribner's Sons, 1914.

Tommy Trot's Visit to Santa Claus. New York: Charles Scribner's Sons, 1908.

Selected Bibliography

Tommy Trot's Visit to Santa Claus and *A Captured Santa Claus.*
New York: Charles Scribner's Sons, 1916.
Two Little Confederates. New York: Charles Scribner's Sons, 1888.
Two Prisoners. New York: R. H. Russell, 1898.
Unc' Edinburg: A Plantation Echo. New York: Charles Scribner's
Sons, 1889.
Under the Crust. New York: Charles Scribner's Sons, 1907.
°*Washington and Its Romance.* New York: Doubleday, Page and
Company, 1923.

2. *Articles*

[All the Geography a Nigger Needs to Know,] *Harper's New Monthly
Magazine,* LXXXV (September, 1892), 642-43.
"The Answer," *Harper's Weekly,* XLII (July, 1898), 750.
"The Bent Monk," *Scribner's Magazine,* XXXIX (June, 1906), 759-60.
"The Bigot," *Scribner's Magazine,* XLVIII (November, 1910), 533-47.
"Billington's Valentine," *Harper's New Monthly Magazine,* LXXXVI
(March, 1893), 642-44.
"Bred in the Bone," *Century,* n.s. LXII (October, 1901), 939-51.
"The Burial of the Guns," *Scribner's Magazine,* XV (April, 1894),
410-22.
"A Captured Santa Claus," *Harper's Young People,* X (December,
1888), 82-88.
"Charlie Whittler's Christmas Party," *Harper's New Monthly
Magazine,* LXXXVI (December, 1892), 155-57.
"The Christmas Peace," *Metropolitan Magazine,* XIX (January, 1904),
[481]-500.
°["The Country Lawyer: An After-Dinner Speech,"] New York State
Bar Association, Proceedings of the Annual Meeting, Albany,
1907, XXX, 391-96.
"The Danger of Being Too Thorough," *Harper's New Monthly
Magazine,* LXXXVI (February, 1893), 482-83.
°"The Democratic Opportunity," *North American,* CXCIII (February,
1911), 193-205.
°"The Disfranchisement of the Negro," *Scribner's Magazine,* XXXVI
(July, 1904), 15-24.
"The Dragon of the Seas," *Washington Post,* April 5, 1898, n.v.
°"The Earthquake in the Abruzzi," *Scribner's Magazine,* LVII
(April, 1915), 219-430.
"Elsket," *Scribner's Magazine,* X (August, 1891), 226-41.
"The Exile," *Scribner's Magazine,* LIII (May, 1913), 654.
°"The First University in America," *Corks and Curls,* XX, University
of Virginia, 1907, 6-10.

*"Francis Hopkinson Smith," *Scribner's Magazine,* LVIII (September, 1915), 304-13.

"General Lee and the Confederate Government," *Scribner's Magazine,* L (November, 1911), 581-92.

"A Gray Jacket," *Century,* n.s. XXII (May, 1892), 27-33.

"The Great-Grandmother's Ghost," *Harper's New Monthly Magazine,* LXXXVII (November, 1893), 966-69.

"He Knew What Was Due to the Court," *Harper's New Monthly Magazine,* (October, 1893), 804-6.

"He Would Have Gotten a Lawyer," *Harper's New Monthly Magazine,* LXXXVII (June, 1893), 155-56.

"Her Sympathetic Editor," *Harper's New Monthly Magazine,* LXXXVII (September, 1893), 642-44.

"The Hostage, or, Along the Potomac: A One-Act Play," *Metropolitan Magazine,* XXIV (September, 1906), 667-81.

*"How Aleck Thompson Played It," *Harper's New Monthly Magazine,* LXXXIX (November, 1894), 966-69.

"How Andrews Carried the Precinct," *Harper's New Monthly Magazine,* LXXXVII (July, 1893), 317-20.

"How Jinny Eased Her Mind," *Harper's New Monthly Magazine,* LXXXVI (May, 1893), 974-76.

["How Isrul Outplayed Gabrul,"] *Harper's New Monthly Magazine,* LXVII (April, 1892), 808-10.

"How the Captain Made Christmas," *Scribner's Magazine,* XIV (December, 1893), 779-86.

"Jack and Jake," *Harper's Young People,* XII (October 13, 20, and 27, 1891), 813-16, 830-33, 846-49.

"Jamestown, the Cradle of American Civilization," *Century,* n.s. LII, 141-50.

"The Jamestown Settlement and Its First Fruit: Civil Liberty," *Outlook,* LXXXVI (May 11, 1907), 59-63.

["Jim and Old Sue"], *Harper's New Monthly Magazine,* LXXXV (July, 1892), 157-58.

*"John Fox," *Scribner's Magazine,* LXVI (December, 1919), 674-83.

"John's Wedding Suit," *Harper's New Monthly Magazine,* LXXXVIII (January, 1894), 320-22.

"Kittykin and the Part She Played in the War," *Harper's Young People,* XII (February 17, 24, 1891), 270-71, 286-88.

*["Lady's Choice,"] *Harper's New Monthly Magazine,* LXXXV (August, 1892), 482-83.

"Leander's Light," *Century,* n.s. LII (June, 1907), 376-85.

"Lee in Defeat," *South Atlantic Quarterly,* V (January, 1907), 1-26.

*Letter to the editor of the *New York Times,* New York, October 26, 1912, "Thomas Nelson Page Out for Gov. Wilson," *New York Times,* Sunday, October 27, 1912, p. 4.

"Literature in the South Before the War," *Lippincott's Magazine,* XLIV (July, 1889), 105-20.

°"Literature in the South Since the War," *Lippincott's Magazine,* XLVIII (December, 1891), 740-56.

"Little Darby," *Scribner's Magazine,* XVI (September and October, 1894), 285-95, 457-71.

["Little Mordicai at the Bar,"] *Harper's New Monthly Magazine,* LXXXIV (May, 1892), 970-72.

"The Long Hillside: A Christmas Hare-Hunt in Old Virginia," *St. Nicholas,* XIX (December, 1891), 106-12.

°["The Loss the Fiduciary Principle,"] New York State Bar Association, Proceedings of the Annual Meeting, Albany, 1907, XXX, 202-28.

"Love Song," *Scribner's Magazine,* XXXVII (January, 1905), 44.

°"The Lynching of Negroes—Its Cause and Its Prevention," *North American Review,* CLXXVII (January, 1904), 33-48.

"Marse Chan," *Century,* XXVII (April, 1884), 932-42.

"Meh Lady," *Century,* XXXII (June, 1886), 187-205.

"Miss Dangerlie's Roses," *Scribner's Magazine,* XII (November, 1892), 650-56.

"Miss Godwin's Inheritance," *Scribner's Magazine,* XXXVI (August, 1904), 171-81.

["Most Worthless Man in Our Class,"] *Harper's New Monthly Magazine,* LXXV (October, 1892), 804-5. (Title in the Plantation Edition is "She Had on Her Geranium Leaves.")

"Nancy Pansy," *Harper's Young People,* XI (December 3, 10, 1889), 83-87, 97-101.

°"A Neglected Class," *Good Housekeeping,* XL (January, 1905), 25-29.

"The New Agent at Lebanon Station," *Ladies' Home Journal,* XXII (April, 1905), 7-8, and (May, 1905), 9-10.

"The Old Dominion," *Harper's New Monthly Magazine,* LXXXVIII (December, 1893), 4-24.

"The Old Gentleman of the Black Stock," *Harper's New Monthly Magazine,* LXXXIX (October, 1894), 774-96.

"Old Jabe's Marital Experiment," *Century,* LXIV (September, 1902), 704.

"Old Yorktown," *Scribner's Monthly,* XXII (October, 1881), 801-16.

"The Old Planters'," *Century,* LXXXVIII (May, 1909), 3-21.

"Ole 'Stracted," *Harper's New Monthly Magazine,* LXXIII (October, 1886), 696-703.

"An Old Virginia Neighborhood," *Metropolitan Magazine,* XXI (December, 1904), 355-63.

"An Old Virginia Sunday," *Scribner's Magazine,* XXX (December, 1901), 727-37.

°"On Changing the Name of the Protestant Episcopal Church," *Churchman*, April 19, 1913, pp. 506-8.

°"On the Decay of Manners," *Century*, LXXXI (April, 1911), 881-87.

"P'Laski's Tunaments," *Harper's New Monthly Magazine*, LXXXII (December, 1890), 111-18.

°"President Roosevelt from the Standpoint of a Southern Democrat," *Metropolitan Magazine*, XXI (March, 1905), 671-81.

"The Prosecution of Mrs. Dullet," *Harper's New Monthly Magazine*, LXXXVI (January, 1893), 320-22.

["Relius,"] *Harper's New Monthly Magazine*, LXXXV (July, 1892), 320-21.

°"The Romantic Founding of Washington," *Scribner's Magazine*, LIV (September, 1913), 319-29.

"Run to Seed," *Scribner's Magazine*, X (August, 1891), 226-41.

"Social Life in Old Virginia Before the War: All the Year and Christmas," *Christian Union*, XLIV (December 19, 1891), 1212-21.

"A Southerner on the Negro Question," *North American Review*, CLIV (April, 1892), 401-13.

"The Southern People During Reconstruction," *Atlantic Monthly*, LXXXVIII (September, 1901), 289-304.

"The Spectre in the Cart," *Scribner's Magazine*, XXVI (August, 1899), 179-90.

°"The Stable of the Inn," *Scribner's Magazine*, LII (December, 1912), 641-47.

"A Story of Charlie Harris," *Harper's New Monthly Magazine*, LXXXVI (April, 1893), 804-5.

°"The Stranger's Pew," *Scribner's Magazine*, XLVIII (December, 1910), 685-89.

"Theocritus on Agradina," *Atlantic Monthly*, XCVIII (August, 1906), 181.

°"Thomas's Baptism," *Scribner's Magazine*, LIV (August, 1913), 204-12.

°"The Trick Doctor," *Scribner's Magazine*, L (September, 1911), 272-83.

"The True Story of the Surrender of Marquis Cornwallis," *Harper's New Monthly Magazine*, LXXXV (November, 1892), 968-69.

Two Little Confederates, *St. Nicholas*, XV (May-October, 1888), 483-90, 571-81, 643-49, 730-38, 804-13, 904-9.

"Two Prisoners," *Harper's Young People*, XIII (May 10, 17, 1892), 481-84, 494-96, 498.

"Unc' Edinburg's Drowndin'," *Harper's New Monthly Magazine*, LXXII (January, 1886), 304-15.

"Uncle Gable's White Folks," *Scribner's Monthly*, XIII (April, 1877), 882.

Selected Bibliography

"The University of Virginia," *Scribner's Magazine*, XXXVII (April, 1905), 396-410.

"Virginians and Constitutional Government," *North American*, CXCVII (March, 1913), 371-91.

"The Voice of the Sea," *Scribner's Magazine*, XX (September, 1901), 363-64.

SECONDARY SOURCES

The following list is rigorously selective. The scholarship on Page is indeed superficial, little more than a few general tributes that were written early in the century. With the exception of Miss Holman's dissertation, no work of consequence has been written on Page since his brother's biography forty years ago.

1. Books

HOLMAN, HARRIET. *The Literary Career of Thomas Nelson Page, 1884-1910*. Unpublished Ph.D. dissertation, Duke University, 1947. Invaluable to the student of Page. Miss Holman, who draws most of her information from the large collection of Page manuscripts at Duke University, has all the important facts of Page's life and milieu. Her interpretation of Page's artistic achievement is sound, and she shows judiciousness and perception in her estimates of individual works. Her thorough bibliography is indispensable.

PAGE, ROSEWELL. *Thomas Nelson Page: A Memoir of a Virginia Gentleman*. New York: Charles Scribner's Sons, 1923. The only published biography of Page. The book is a sympathetic portrait, with interesting details that often are of a "quasi-historical" nature. The faith one might ordinarily have in the work is marred by Rosewell Page's tendency to eulogize his brother's life.

2. Essays

CABLE, GEORGE W. "Thomas Nelson Page, a Study in Reminiscence and Appreciation," *The Book News Monthly*, XVIII (November, 1909), 139-40. A frankly personal essay which is really a eulogy.

HUBBELL, JAY BROADUS. *The South in American Literature*. Durham: Duke University Press, 1954. A good short account of Page's life and work which relates Page to his historical context.

—————. *Southern Life in Fiction*. Athens: University of Georgia Press, 1960. An excellent brief background to Southern literature as it "reflects the life of the American people." Hubbell places Page in his proper literary tradition.

————. *"Virginia Life in Fiction," American Literature.* New York: New York Public Library, 1922. The sanest early estimation of Page's role in Virginian and American fiction. Hubbell calls *In Ole Virginia* "preeminently the Virginia classic."

MIMS, EDWIN. "Thomas Nelson Page," *Southern Writers,* II (Nashville, 1903), 120-51. Favorable, persuasive account of Page's achievement. Valuable for some information not to be found elsewhere.

QUINN, ARTHUR HOBSON. *American Fiction, An Historical and Critical Survey.* New York: Appleton-Century Company, Inc., 1936. Very sympathetic, although Quinn is not blind to Page's limitations in *Gordon Keith* and in *John Marvel.* Quinn accepts too readily Page's version of the ante-bellum South and Reconstruction. He includes two interesting letters sent to him by Page; one refers to *Little Darby* and the other to *Red Rock.*

WILSON, EDMUND. *Patriotic Gore.* New York: Oxford University Press, 1962. A brief, sensible account of Page as a writer who represents the Southern position in the late nineteenth century. Wilson contrasts Page's views of the Negro with those of Cable.

Index

Index